DEVIL'S ADVOCATES

DEVIL'S ADVOCATES is a series of books devoted to exploring the classics of horror cinema. Contributors to the series come from the fields of teaching, academia, journalism and fiction, but all have one thing in common: a passion for the horror film and a desire to share it with the widest possible audience.

'The admirable Devil's Advocates series is not only essential – and fun – reading for the serious horror fan but should be set texts on any genre course.'
Dr Ian Hunter, Professor of Film Studies, De Montfort University, Leicester

'Auteur Publishing's new Devil's Advocates critiques on individual titles... offer bracingly fresh perspectives from passionate writers. The series will perfectly complement the BFI archive volumes.' **Christopher Fowler,** *Independent on Sunday*

'Devil's Advocates has proven itself more than capable of producing impassioned, intelligent analyses of genre cinema... quickly becoming the go-to guys for intelligent, easily digestible film criticism.' **Horror Talk.com**

'Auteur Publishing continue the good work of giving serious critical attention to significant horror films.' **Black Static**

 DevilsAdvocatesbooks

DevilsAdBooks

ALSO AVAILABLE IN THIS SERIES

Antichrist Amy Simmonds

Black Sunday Martyn Conterio

The Blair Witch Project Peter Turner

Candyman Jon Towlson

Cannibal Holocaust Calum Waddell

Carrie Neil Mitchell

The Company of Wolves James Gracey

Creepshow Simon Brown

The Curse of Frankenstein Marcus K. Harmes

Dead of Night Jez Conolly & David Bates

The Descent James Marriot

The Devils Darren Arnold

Don't Look Now Jessica Gildersleeve

The Fly Emma Westwood

Frenzy Ian Cooper

Halloween Murray Leeder

House of Usher Evert Jan van Leeuwen

In the Mouth of Madness Michael Blyth

It Follows Joshua Grimm

Ju-on The Grudge Marisa C. Hayes

Let the Right One In Anne Billson

M Samm Deighan

Macbeth Rebekah Owens

Nosferatu Cristina Massaccesi

Saw Benjamin Poole

Scream Steven West

The Shining Laura Mee

The Silence of the Lambs Barry Forshaw

Suspiria Alexandra Heller-Nicholas

The Texas Chain Saw Massacre James Rose

The Thing Jez Conolly

Twin Peaks: Fire Walk With Me Lindsay Hallam

Witchfinder General Ian Cooper

FORTHCOMING

Blood and Black Lace Roberto Curti

Daughters of Darkness Kat Ellinger

Peeping Tom Kiri Walden

[REC] Jim Harper

Shivers Luke Aspell

Devil's Advocates

The Mummy

Doris V. Sutherland

Acknowledgments

I have drawn heavily on the past work of other horror historians, but none more so than Philip J. Riley. Thanks to Riley's decades-long publishing work, I was able to read the original shooting script of *The Mummy* along with documents from its earlier incarnation as *Cagliostro*, all of which played vital roles in my research.

This book is dedicated to the Horror Honeys, who had to put up with my puns. That's a wrap, ladies!

First published in 2019 by
Auteur, 24 Hartwell Crescent, Leighton Buzzard LU7 1NP
www.auteur.co.uk
Copyright © Auteur 2019

Series design: Nikki Hamlett at Cassels Design
Set by Cassels Design www.casselsdesign.co.uk

All rights reserved. No part of this publication may be reproduced in any material form (including photocopying or storing in any medium by electronic means and whether or not transiently or incidentally to some other use of this publication) without the permission of the copyright owner.

British Library Cataloguing-in-Publication Data
A catalogue record for this book is available from the British Library

ISBN paperback: 978-1-911325-95-6
ISBN ebook: 978-1-911325-96-3

Contents

Introduction 7

Part 1: Origins

Chapter 1. Literary Precursors 15

Chapter 2. From Cagliostro to Imhotep: The Writing Process 29

Chapter 3. The Makers of *The Mummy* 43

Part 2: Analysis

Chapter 4. The Egypt of *The Mummy* 55

Chapter 5. Horror and Fantasy in *The Mummy* 73

Part 3: Unwrapping

Chapter 6. Conversations with *The Mummy*: Critical Reactions 87

Chapter 7. The Legacy of *The Mummy* 97

Conclusion 111

Bibliography 119

INTRODUCTION

Fig 1: Original release poster for The Mummy

In the early weeks of 1933, a wizened face glared down from the glowing lights of Broadway's RKO Mayfair cinema. With hollow cheeks, blank eyes, heavy brows and an unreadable expression, this sinister visage dared passers-by to enter the darkened building.

The owner of the face was identified as Karloff the Uncanny, a moniker suggesting a stage magician more than a film actor. Indeed, the associated promotional pieces evoked a conjuring trick, a magic spectacle, an alchemical transformation. 'It comes to life', proclaimed many of them, while others went into more detail: 'Buried alive, brought back to life again 3700 years later!' 'You'll hardly believe what your own eyes see!' 'Yesterday a mummy; today a living breathing, fighting MAN…'[1]

The subject of this alluring campaign was a film that enjoyed a limited release in December 1932 before receiving general distribution the following month: *The Mummy*. It was the latest venture into the macabre from Universal Pictures, the studio that maintained a reputation as Hollywood's bastion of horror. In the silent era Universal produced films starring Lon Chaney, whose skill at creating grotesque make-up earned him the sobriquet of the Man of a Thousand Faces. Chaney had died in 1930, but this did not deter Universal from continuing to explore the potential of horror cinema. The sound era had brought with it *Dracula* (1931), *Frankenstein* (1931), *Murders in the Rue Morgue* (1932) and *The Old Dark House* (1932).

Other studios were waking up to the potential of horror. Production Code administrator Jason S. Joy expressed concern about the new wave of horror films, and asked Motion Pictures Producers and Distributors of America president Will Hays (later to find infamy as the creator of the Hays Code) if films such as Universal's *Dracula* and *Frankenstein*, along with Paramount's *Dr. Jekyll and Mr. Hyde* (1931), marked 'the beginning of a cycle that ought to be retarded or killed'. Meanwhile, the 1 August 1932 edition of trade paper *Film Daily* ran the front-page headline 'Schedules Show Cycle of "Horror" Picture Continuing', as Paramount's *Island of Lost Souls* (1932) and RKO's *King Kong* (1933) went into production.[2]

It was Universal's films, particularly *Dracula* and *Frankenstein*, that broadened the horizons of Hollywood horror. Where silent spooks such as the vampire of *London After Midnight* (1927) or the devil of *Seven Footprints to Satan* (1929) would be unmasked as mortals in disguise,[3] Universal horror of the 1930s showed few qualms about full-blown supernatural and Gothic subjects. Vampires could rise from coffins to suck blood, while fragments of grave-robbed corpses could be stitched together into a rampaging monster. Now, an ancient Egyptian mummy was coming to life before the startled eyes of the audience!

In some ways, *The Mummy* offered filmgoers the sort of material that they would have come to expect from this new wave of screen horror; that the opening credits are set to the same strains of *Swan Lake* that introduced *Dracula* and *Murders in the Rue Morgue* may have been reassuringly familiar. But in other respects the film marked a departure. Universal's previous horror films had generally taken place against a European backdrop informed by English Gothic and German Expressionism; *The Mummy*, on the other hand, turned to Egypt and its ancient history for inspiration. In doing so, the film hit upon what was, as far as cinema was concerned, a fresh variety of monster: a living mummy.

Previous films had approached this concept only in indirect, uncertain terms. For example, the short trickfilms of French magician-turned-filmmaker Georges Méliès and his British counterpart Walter R. Booth created images of Egyptian dead returning to life as a means of amazing audiences of early cinema with trick photography. In Méliès' *Robbing Cleopatra's Tomb* (*Cléopâtre*, 1899) a man dismembers a mummy and burns its pieces to summon a living Cleopatra, while *The Monster* (*Le Monstre*, 1903) has an Egyptian magician turn a skeleton into a white-shrouded ghost and then into an Egyptian maiden. In Booth's *The Haunted Curiosity Shop* (1902), meanwhile, a sarcophagus becomes a live Egyptian and then an armoured knight.

Other films rationalised the supernatural with plots about people disguising themselves as mummies. *Die Augen der Mumie Ma* (*Eyes of the Mummy*, 1918) gets its name from a brief scene in which a mummy appears to open its eyes, but this turns out to be someone looking through a pair of peepholes in a fake sarcophagus. The idea also appeared in comedies such as *The Egyptian Mummy* (1912) and *For the Love of Tut* (1923), while *The Mask of Fu Manchu* (Karloff's previous film of 1932) has the henchmen of the Chinese villain disguise themselves as mummies as they carry out a kidnapping in a museum. Meanwhile, Walt Disney had revived mummies for comic purposes in the 1931 cartoon *Egyptian Melodies*, where four mummies hop out of their sarcophagi and dance about as best they can with their limbs bound; a sight gag reveals that their embalmers have thoughtfully granted them button-up seat flaps in the manner of full-body pyjamas. Of these films, none can be said to have put the image of the living mummy to full effect.

Thanks to *The Mummy*, however, the cloth-wrapped Egyptian revenant would join the vampire, the werewolf and Frankenstein's Monster as a horror icon, one that would appear in innumerable sequels, imitations and parodies. This film from 1932 is where the living mummy began his eerie shamble across the imaginations of the filmgoing public.

THE PLOT OF *THE MUMMY*

The film begins in Egypt, 1921. Three archaeologists working for the British Museum discuss their latest discoveries: the mummy of an ancient Egyptian named Imhotep, and a mysterious sealed box. The youngest of the three reacts with vulgar enthusiasm, but the two older men argue amongst themselves. One, Sir Joseph Whemple, feels that these artefacts will benefit human understanding; the other, resident occult expert Dr. Muller, is more apprehensive. He believes that the box contains the Scroll of Thoth, an artefact said to hold dangerous powers, and he argues that it would have been better off buried.

While the two elders head elsewhere to argue, the younger archaeologist opens the box and reads from the scroll inside. As he does so, the mummy opens its eyes and steps out of its sarcophagus. At the sight of the living mummy, which picks up the scroll and departs, the young man goes insane. When Muller and Whemple return, they find the artefacts missing and their young comrade overcome with hysterical laughter.

In 1932, the British Museum holds another field expedition in Egypt. Amongst the archaeologists present is Frank Whemple, son of Sir Joseph Whemple. The expedition prepares to depart after failing to make any significant finds, only for a mysterious fez-clad Egyptian to approach them with unexpected information. Introducing himself as Ardath Bey, he points a location where – so he informs them – they will find the tomb of Princess Anck-es-en-Amon.

Sure enough they find the sealed tomb, and transport the princess' mummy to the Cairo Museum. There, Ardath Bey comes to see the remains of Anck-es-en-Amon, and remains hidden away inside even after the museum closes. He begins chanting the princess' name as he pores over a scroll… the missing Scroll of Thoth.

Meanwhile, a young woman named Helen Grosvenor is staying at a hotel in Cairo; her father is the governor of Sudan, while her mother is from an old Egyptian family. She somehow hears Ardath Bey's chants, and begins walking away as though in a trance. She catches a taxi to the museum; inside, she chants in an ancient Egyptian tongue, sometimes repeating the name of Imhotep. When she reaches the museum and finds it to be closed, she listlessly bangs on the door until she collapses. Frank Whemple finds her and takes her to his home as she continues to chant in her sleep.

Back at the museum, Ardath Bey is caught by a security guard; he manages to kill the guard but leaves the Scroll of Thoth behind in the confusion. The next day Frank Whemple tends to Helen, falling in love with her in the process. Meanwhile, Dr. Muller and the elder Whemple head to the museum. There, they see the guard's body and the nearby Scroll of Thoth, which they take back with them.

Ardath Bey gains access to the Whemples' home by controlling the mind of the household's Nubian servant. Helen becomes fascinated by this visitor, but Muller sends her back to the hotel for her own safety. He then confronts Ardath Bey, making it clear that he knows the Egyptian's secret: Ardath Bey is none other than Imhotep, last seen as a bandaged mummy but subsequently restored through magic.

Ardath Bey – or, rather, Imhotep – returns to his lair, a small building decked out with ancient Egyptian trappings. Staring into a pool, he conjures up images of the Whemples' home. He watches as Sir Joseph Whemple prepares to burn the Scroll of Thoth, under Muller's orders. Using dark magic, Imhotep causes Whemple to suffer a fatal heart attack. The Nubian servant, still under Imhotep's control, retrieves the Scroll of Thoth from the fireplace.

Frank Whemple finds his father's body, and Muller informs him about the supernatural dangers he faces. He gives Frank a charm in the shape of the goddess Isis, telling him that it will protect him. He states that Helen is not in immediate danger, as Imhotep loves her; it is Frank, Helen's protector, whom Imhotep sees as a threat.

Meanwhile, Imhotep takes Helen to his hideout. He shows her to his magic pool, where he conjures up images of ancient Egypt. As he does so, Imhotep narrates the story of his life and death. He explains that he was in love with the princess Anck-es-en-Amon, of whom Helen is a reincarnation. After the princess died young, Imhotep tried to resurrect her using the Scroll of Thoth; he was caught performing this sacrilegious deed and sentenced to be buried alive, the scroll interred with him to prevent any further misuse. The magic hieroglyphs on his sarcophagus were chipped off, barring him from the afterlife. Now, with Imhotep resurrected and Anck-es-en-Amon reincarnated, they can finally be together.

Helen watches the proceedings in a trance before being awakened by Imhotep. She is only dimly aware of what she has witnessed, and speaks of having seen ancient Egypt in a dream. She returns to Frank Whemple and gives him a garbled account of what she has just witnessed. She goes on to exhibit mood swings resulting from

Imhotep's attempts to manipulate her mind from afar. Her strength is sapped as she struggles against the magic, and Muller decides that she can be saved only through the destruction of Imhotep.

At night Imhotep uses his deadly magic on the sleeping Frank, as he had previously done to Joseph Whemple. Frank staggers over to the protective charm of Isis that he had placed over Helen's door and grabs it, saving himself but leaving Helen unprotected. As Frank lies unconscious on the ground, Imhotep compels Helen to head back to the museum where he awaits her.

Helen then recovers to find herself at the museum, dressed in an ancient Egyptian costume. She now has the mind of the princess Anck-es-en-Amon, and is confused by her new location. Imhotep explains to her that her soul is in a new body, and burns her mummy to illustrate this point. He then reveals that he will have her embalmed, allowing her to become immortal as he is.

Her two psyches become conflicted, but Helen/Anck-es-en-Amon finally turns against her former lover Imhotep. Meanwhile, Muller finds the unconscious Frank Whemple and revives him. They head off to the museum together, having realised what Imhotep has in store for Helen.

When they arrive, Imhotep is trying to stab Helen with an ancient knife to begin the embalming process. He wards off the interlopers with his magic; while he is distracted, Helen/Anck-es-en-Amon prays to a statue of Isis. The statue raises its arm, and an ankh in its hand shoots out a blast of lightning. The Scroll of Thoth burns to ashes, while Imhotep first reverts to his mummified state before his face crumbles away, leaving only a skull. Frank embraces Helen as she regains consciousness, the dusty remains of Imhotep lying on the floor.

Horror in Egypt

While the setting and concepts of *The Mummy* were relatively new to horror cinema as it existed in 1932, the film's creative team nonetheless had plenty of sources from which to take inspiration. For more than a century, innumerable writers and visual artists had been drawing upon the history, mythology and iconography of ancient Egypt to create works of romance, fantasy, and sometimes fear. *The Mummy* processed this source material into an enduring classic of cinema.

This book will take a close look at what happened when Hollywood horror went to Egypt.

FOOTNOTES

1. Riley, P. (ed.) *The Mummy* (MagicImage Filmbooks, Absecon, 1989) pp32-3, 51-5
2. Peirse, A., *After Dracula: The 1930s Horror Film* (I. B. Tauris, London, 2013) p7
3. This convention did not exist worldwide, as evidenced by German films such as *Nosferatu* (1922) that portrayed supernatural themes directly.

PART 1: ORIGINS
CHAPTER 1. LITERARY PRECURSORS

Universal's classic horror films were typically adapted from novels, short stories or stage plays. By the time *The Mummy* was released, the studio had already filmed adaptations of Bram Stoker (*Dracula*, 1931), Mary Shelley (*Frankenstein*, 1931), Gaston Leroux (*The Phantom of the Opera*, 1925), Victor Hugo (*The Hunchback of Notre Dame*, 1923; *The Man Who Laughs*, 1928), Edgar Allan Poe (*Murders in the Rue Morgue*, 1932), J. B. Priestley (*The Old Dark House*, 1932) and John Willard (*The Cat and the Canary*, 1927). *The Mummy* was not adapted from a specific text, but it did borrow recognisable elements from weird fiction.

While not necessarily the basis of a coherent subgenre, mummies were a recurring theme in the supernatural literature of the nineteenth and early twentieth centuries as authors of the fantastic found their imaginations fired by the latest developments in Egyptology. Stories from this period often differ significantly from the mummy films that would later develop in Hollywood, but certain aspects of them are nonetheless echoed by Universal's subgenre-defining 1932 film.

HAUNTED MUMMIES

An early, influential mummy story was Théophile Gautier's 'The Mummy's Foot' ('Le Pied de momie', 1840). This was inspired by an illustration in Baron Vivant Denon's 1817 book *Travels in Lower and Upper Egypt* (*Voyage dans la Basse et Haute Egypte*), depicting a mummified foot that Denon found in a tomb during Napoleon's expedition to Egypt.[4] Denon was not alone in taking such momentos: another French writer, Gustave Flaubert, likewise owned the foot of an Egyptian mummy, which he kept on his desk.[5]

Modern observers may balk at the idea of human remains ending up merely as exotic souvenirs, but this was a time when ground-up mummies were still being used as fertiliser, medicine, and painting pigments, a practice that had been going on since the middle ages.[6] In earlier literature of the fantastic, including Shakespeare's *Macbeth* and William Beckford's 1786 Gothic novel *Vathek*, mummies are no more than disposable

15

ingredients for black magic.[7] Gautier is more sensitive than this. His story weaves a poignant afterlife fantasy to remind readers that those mummies were – like the skull of Yorick in *Hamlet* – once living people, with an ironic element in that the mummies end up observing a modern man, rather than vice versa.

Gautier's protagonist purchases the mummified foot of one Princess Hermonthis from an antique dealer to use as a paperweight. At night, he falls asleep surrounded by the scent of the foot's embalming mixture and experiences a vivid dream. First he witnesses the foot coming to life, leaping frog-like over his papers. Next, the princess herself arrives, clad in a skirt made from mummy wrappings; other than lacking her foot, she possesses 'the purest Egyptian type of perfect beauty'. Once the narrator restores her lost appendage, she takes him to an underground hallway peopled with mummified pharaohs – some contemporaries of Noah, some older even than Adam – who offer him a reward for his deed, only for him to be rudely awoken.

It would be a stretch to call 'The Mummy's Foot' a horror story. The revenants that appear in the narrator's dream are more dignified than disturbing; Gautier describes them as being 'dry, withered, wrinkled like parchment, and blackened with naphtha and bitumen', but this mummified state is ultimately used to emphasise their age and gravitas.

Gautier's piece prefigured a cycle of ghost stories about mummies. H. Rider Haggard's 1912 story 'Smith and the Pharaohs' hits many of the same narrative beats as 'The Mummy's Foot': an archaeologist becomes infatuated with the image of a beautiful Egyptian queen; he falls asleep in the company of mummies; he dreams of being surrounded by ancient Egyptian personages; and the object of his affections pleads his case before the Pharaohs. Edging away from afterlife fantasy and towards horror fiction we find a 1912 story by Jessie Adelaide Middleton, also called 'The Mummy's Foot'. Here, a group of partygoers pass around the mummified foot of an Egyptian dancer as a curiosity. One of the women attending the party takes the foot home as a good luck charm, an act that the story's narrator finds appalling: 'I think that to carry portions of an embalmed body about, however long ago they may have been entombed, is not only irreverent, but is downright desecration.'

'Also,' the storyteller adds, 'I have known queer things about mummies and mummy influence'. Sure enough, the woman is forced to discard the foot once she begins feeling an intangible presence around her house. We then learn that the foot's discoverer has a story of his own: while he was living in a rented room, the child of his landlady had complained of seeing 'a black naked foot peeping in and out from under the curtain of the kitchen dresser downstairs... as if it was dancing'.

Another narrative that uses a mummy as a haunted artefact can be found in Elliott O'Donnell's 1911 book *Byways of Ghost-Land*, a dubious compendium of allegedly true ghost stories. In one of these accounts a Frenchman travels to Thebes and finds the mummy of a woman named Met-Om-Karema, which he decides to take as a souvenir. Spending the night in a tent on his way back through the desert, he wakes to see the mummy alive and breathing. It begins to slowly unwrap itself; underneath the bandages is not an ancient Egyptian but the Frenchman's mother, who died during his childhood. He falls to his knees and kisses her feet, only to find that the apparition of his mother has undergone a transformation into 'the fleshless, mouldering face of a foul and barely recognisable corpse'. As he flees from the tent, he sees that the mummy has been lying on the floor the whole time. The apparition vanishes as the Frenchman's servants arrive on the scene. Early cinema also used the mummy-as-haunted-artefact concept: *The Avenging Hand* (1915) has an Egyptian ghost return for her mummified hand, echoing the mummy's foot stories by Gautier and Middleton.

WALKING MUMMIES

The central image of mummy movies – that of the mummy coming back to life like a bandaged zombie – is absent from all of the above stories. Prior to the release of *The Mummy* in 1932, the animated mummy was not a particularly common theme in weird fiction, although it can be found across a modest smattering of stories.

Years before Gautier created his ghostly princess, Jane Loudon had penned a very different treatment of the mummy theme. Published in 1827, *The Mummy! A Tale of the Twenty-Second Century* is a science fiction saga influenced by Mary Shelley's *Frankenstein* (1818). In it, a scientist uses galvanism to resurrect a mummified Egyptian named Cheops in the year 2126; Cheops promptly runs amok in England, even killing the Queen.[8] The novel portrays the mummy as being in a remarkably good state of preservation:

> All was perfect as though life still animated the form before them, and it had only reclined there to seek a short repose. The dark eyebrows, the thick raven hair which hung upon the forehead and the snow-white teeth seen through the half-open lips, forbade the idea of death...

Loudon's mummy is less a resurrected corpse and more a man who has come out of suspended animation, like Washington Irving's Rip Van Winkle. This concept also turns up in Edgar Allen Poe's humorous 1845 story 'Some Words with a Mummy', where assembled Egyptologists unwrap the mummy of an individual named Allamistakeo – who once again turns out to be in such good condition that it takes only an electric shock to bring him to life. The revived Allamistakeo is thoroughly unimpressed with the modern world of the nineteenth century, while the narrator ends up deciding to be embalmed for a couple of centuries in turn. The plot device of galvanism made it into early mummy cinema, with a 1911 short film entitled *The Mummy* depicting a female mummy being revived by electricity and marrying an Egyptologist.

These stories, where mummification is a form of suspended animation, are extreme examples of a motif also found in Gauter's story: the image of the mummy as a perfectly preserved body, often so perfect as to be beautiful, as when Gautier describes Hermonthis' foot in prettified terms as 'slender and delicate... perfectly formed'. His later story *The Romance of a Mummy* (*Le Roman de la momie*, 1858), where the mummy lacks a supernatural aspect and is used as part of a framing device for a tale set in the Egypt of Moses, likewise portrays mummification is a thing of beauty:

> The last wrapping taken off, the young woman showed in the chaste nudity of her lovely form, preserving, in spite of so many centuries that had passed away, the fullness of her contours, and the easy grace of her pure lines. Her pose, an infrequent one in the case of mummies, was that of the Venus of Medici, as if the embalmers had wished to save this beautiful body from the set attitude of death and to soften the inflexible rigidity of the cadaver.

Gautier would not see a mummy in person until the World Exhibition was held in Paris in 1867. His account of this sight was much less idealised:

> Her enamelled eyes gazed fixedly and terrifyingly ahead, her nose was pushed back at the tip in order to conceal the incision through which her brain had been extracted from her skull; gold leaf sealed her lips. Her trunk revealed reddish skin which developed a blue bloom when it came into contact with the air, like mould on pictures, and in her side could be seen the incision which served to allow the removal of her entrails and from which escaped a trail of aromatic sawdust mixed with resin in small grains resembling colophony, as if it were stuffing from a broken doll.[9]

With this description in mind, it is hard to imagine the resurrection of a mummy as anything other than a thing of horror. Mary Shelley did not show an idealised conception of the embalming process when she had Victor Frankenstein proclaim, upon seeing his creation, that 'A mummy again endued with animation could not be so hideous as that wretch'. William Call Spencer invoked similar imagery in 'The Green God' (1916), where the main character encounters the mummified corpse of a miner and imagines it coming to life:

> In the quivering light the twisted limbs appeared to move and contort. The green skin upon the skull, drawn back until the cruel mouth grinned insanely, the hollowed cheeks, the deep eye-sockets that stared at him, the taut, glistening parchment upon the forehead—these fascinated the sailor so that he could not look away. He expected it to stand over him to point its skinny, withered arm at him or to open its jaws, in a shattering laugh.

Arthur Conan Doyle was another author who was aware of the ghoulish potential offered by the image of the walking mummy, but he approached it in a very different way to Shelley and Spencer. Doyle's 1892 short story 'Lot No. 249' introduces readers to a group of Oxford students; one, Edward Bellingham, is a keen Egyptologist and owns an Egyptian mummy: 'a horrid, black, withered thing, like a charred head on a gnarled bush, was lying half out of the case, with its clawlike hand and bony forearm resting upon the table'. After a series of unexplained events, ranging from strange behaviour on the part of Bellingham to attacks on the students by an unseen assailant, protagonist Abercrombie Smith becomes convinced that Bellingham is bringing the mummy to life through magical means and forcing it to do his bidding.

The story is ultimately interested more in English eccentricity than Egyptian mysticism, and the formula of the mummy movie – as it would later develop – is not *quite* in place here. Following an established convention of the ghost story, Doyle is careful to avoid describing the living mummy in clear terms. He instead leaves its activities to the reader's imagination, in contrast to films that would use the shambling mummy as a central image. The story also plays with rationalised supernatural, as the protagonist ignores mundane explanations for the phenomena and becomes increasingly unhinged as he tries to thwart the mummified menace; he eventually forces Bellingham at gunpoint to burn both the mummy and an accompanying papyrus, destroying any potential proof of occult happenings. But despite this, 'Lot No. 249' is perhaps the closest literary predecessor to the stereotyped mummy of Hollywood that arose after the 1932 *Mummy*. Surprisingly, the story has been adapted for the screen only twice: first in 1967 as a now-lost episode of the BBC series *Sir Arthur Conan Doyle*, and later as part of the 1990 anthology film *Tales from the Darkside: The Movie*.

Under their pseudonyms of E. and H. Heron, Katherine and Hesketh Prichard explored similar territory when they pitted their occult detective Flaxman Low against a mummy in 'The Story of Baelbrow' (1899). In this story, the owner of an English mansion purchases an Egyptian mummy only to find that the building was already haunted by a ghost – a *vampiric* ghost, no less. The spirit finds a new home in the mummy, animating the dried old body and draining the blood of the mansion's occupants. Like Doyle, the Prichards portray their mummy as an ambiguous, intangible presence glimpsed out of the corner of the eye, a sign of the narrative's roots in the ghost story tradition.

'The Story of Baelbrow' is unusual in that it completely avoids the exotic trappings of Egypt and instead has its mummy animated by a spirit that haunts English soil. At the opposite end of the spectrum we find the 1924 *Weird Tales* story 'Imprisoned with the Pharaohs' – originally presented as an autobiographical work by Harry Houdini, but actually ghost-written by H. P. Lovecraft[10] – which goes all-out in depicting Egypt as a land of dark folklore. 'Perhaps the most leeringly blood-congealing legends', comments the narrator, 'are those which relate to certain perverse products of decadent priestcraft—composite mummies made by the artificial union of human trunks and limbs with the heads of animals in imitation of the elder gods.' Lovecraft avoids portraying supernatural phenomena in literal terms – the tale was presented as a true story, after all – and allows the animal-headed mummies to live only in the fevered dreams and imaginings of the story's narrator:

> The training of unhallowed thousands of years must lie behind that march of earth's inmost monstrosities… padding, clicking, walking, stalking, rumbling, lumbering, crawling… and all to the abhorrent discords of those mocking instruments. And then—God keep the memory of those Arab legends out of my head!—the mummies without souls…the meeting-place of the wandering kas… the hordes of the devil-cursed pharaonic dead of forty centuries… the composite mummies led through the uttermost onyx voids by King Khephren and his ghoul-queen Nitocris...

Jeffery Farnol's 1929 tale 'Black Coffee', while little-known, may be the quintessential work of mummy horror as it existed before Universal's film. The story combines a set of recurring themes: the mummy as haunted artefact; the concept of the walking mummy; and the ancient curse, a topic that will be covered later in this book. 'Black Coffee' revolves around a professor – in a state of agitation due to overconsumption of the titular beverage – acquiring an Egyptian mummy. Once again it is perfectly preserved, but this time it is not a thing of beauty. It is instead the devilish-looking body of an infamous princess named Ahasuera, and is accompanied by a curse: 'Isis awhile hath stayed my breath/Whoso wakes me shall find death.' The nervous professor is terrified of the mummy, which finally comes to life and gives him a fatal heart attack. His own dead body is found with the mummy inexplicably draped over it.

The nightmarish mummies described by Lovecraft and Farnol form an opposite archetype to the beautiful, melancholy mummies of Théophile Gautier. Both of these archetypes are on show in The Mummy: the former represented by Imhotep, the latter embodied by Anck-es-en-Amon, and the drama between the two characters deriving from their contrast.

DIRECT PRECURSORS

While each of the authors discussed above contributed to the portrayal of mummies and ancient Egypt in fantastic literature, there are three writers in particular who stand out as the most likely influences upon Universal's *The Mummy*: Bram Stoker, Arthur Conan Doyle and H. Rider Haggard.

Fig 2: 1925 She poster

As discussed elsewhere in this book, The Mummy owes a considerable amount to Universal's adaptation of Dracula, meaning that the indirect influence of Bram Stoker permeates the film. On a more subtle level The Mummy may well have taken inspiration from Stoker's 1903 novel The Jewel of Seven Stars, which remains almost certainly the best-known mummy story of classic weird fiction.

The Jewel of Seven Stars combines the mummy-as-haunted-artefact theme with the concept of the perfectly-preserved mummy. The novel begins with an Egyptologist being found inexplicably unconscious amongst his collection of artefacts – including the seven-fingered hand of Tera, an Egyptian sorceress erased from historical record for her blasphemous pursuit of eternal life. Stoker may have based this character partly upon Hatshepsut, the female pharaoh whose name was removed from her monuments after her death by her stepson, Thutmose III.[11] The novel also establishes that Tera's coffin texts barred her from the afterlife – a fate that was later suffered by Universal's Imhotep.

Multiple mummies show signs of life throughout the novel, although their activities occur off the page. One character is apparently strangled by the severed hand, another seemingly scratched by the mummified remains of Tera's cat. In the original edition of the novel the heroine Margaret – who turns out to be Tera's reincarnation – has her soul transferred back into the pristine mummy after a climactic ritual; the book was later reprinted with a more upbeat conclusion, although whether this was Stoker's doing remains unknown.

The Jewel of Seven Stars is relevant to *The Mummy* because, in each case, the heroine is a reincarnation of an ancient Egyptian woman, and is faced with the prospect of regaining the memories and personality of her earlier self. During the climax, Margaret expresses anguish at the thought of Tera's mummy being unwrapped:

> 'Father, you are not going to unswathe her! All you men...! And in the glare of light!'
>
> 'But why not, my dear?'
>
> 'Just think, Father, a woman! All alone! In such a way! In such a place! Oh! it's cruel, cruel!'

This exchange is echoed in *The Mummy*, when Frank speaks to Helen about unwrapping the body of Anck-es-en-Amon:

> 'When we came to unwrap the girl herself...'
>
> 'How could you do that?'
>
> 'We had to! Science, you know! Well, after we'd worked amongst her things, I felt as though I'd known her. When we got the wrappings off and I saw her face, you'll think me silly, but I sort of fell in love with her.'

Frank then realises Helen's resemblance to Anck-es-en-Amon's mummy. Meanwhile, in *The Jewel of Seven Stars*, the unwrapping of Tera reveals her to have been identical to Margaret.

Some aspects of the novel are closer to the February 1932 Nina Wilcox Putnam script (discussed in the following chapter of this book) than to the final film. Putnam's script, like *The Jewel of Seven Stars*, is awash with the influence of early twentieth-century spiritualism, and the two texts use similar terminology in describing the supernatural. The characters in Stoker's novel dub their attempt to resurrect Queen Tera as their 'Great Experiment', a phrase which is used as the title of the final chapter; Putnam's script likewise has its characters refer to the climactic ritual as an 'experiment'. In the finished film, the ritual has become 'the great change'.

The next author of note is Arthur Conan Doyle. As discussed above, Doyle's 'Lot No. 249' has similarities to later mummy movies; but as far as the 1932 film is concerned, his most relevant work is the short story 'The Ring of Thoth' (1890).

This story begins with John Vansittart Smith, a student of Egyptology, catching sight of a strange man poring over mummies in the Louvre. Smith then falls asleep and awakes after dark to witness the stranger unwrapping a mummy. This turns out to be another one of those perfectly-preserved mummies of romance, with 'a cascade of long, black glossy tresses… a low, white forehead… bright, deeply fringed eyes… a sweet, full, sensitive mouth, and a beautifully curved chin'. The man kisses and embraces the long-dead woman, before conducting an arcane process involving an ancient ring and unknown liquid.

The stranger then notices Smith watching him. He confronts the protagonist with a knife before realising that the female mummy behind him has started to wither. 'The old curse is broken,' says the man after a moment of despair. 'I can rejoin her. What matter about her inanimate shell so long as her spirit is awaiting me at the other side of the veil!'

Showing a change in mood, the stranger leads Smith into a room adorned with ancient art. Giving his name as Sosra, he reveals that he is an Egyptian, but 'not one of the down-trodden race of slaves who now inhabit the Delta of the Nile'. Rather, he was born during the reign of Tuthmosis, sixteen hundred years before Christ. An occultist, he had gone looking for the secret of immortality and developed a chemical substance which, when injected into his blood, allowed him to live for thousands of years. He fell in love with a woman named Atma, only for her to die of plague before he could inject her with his chemicals. Since then, he has sought suicide, something that could only be achieved through a specific poison found in the ring of Thoth. Now, after all these centuries, he has found both the ring and the remains of his lost love Atma, and so prepares to join her in the afterlife.

When comparing 'The Ring of Thoth' to *The Mummy*, it is hard to see Doyle's story as anything other than a sizeable chunk of the raw material that Universal used to fashion the film. It has the tragic Egyptian love between a woman doomed to die, and a man fated to survive into another age; it has sinister goings-on in the Egyptian wing of a museum; and it has immortality achieved through chemical injections, a device found in Nina Wilcox Putnam's Cagliostro script. Indeed, Doyle's description of the millennia-old Egyptian reads like an account of Karloff in character as Ardath Bey: Sosra has skin 'as glazed and as shiny as varnished parchment' but 'cross-hatched by a million delicate wrinkles', while his reptilian eyes give 'a sense of power, of wisdom… and of weariness'. On another level, the film manages to recreate the darkly melancholy atmosphere that is so thick in Doyle's story. If *The Mummy* is an adaptation of 'The Ring of Thoth' then it is a remarkably faithful one in spirit, albeit not necessarily in letter.

Finally we come to H. Rider Haggard, an author best known for his imperialist adventure stories. Haggard touched upon the mummy theme in the aforementioned *Smith and the Pharaohs*, and his historical novel *Cleopatra* (1889) – in which an Egyptian priest is buried alive for offending the gods – also deserves a mention in relation to *The Mummy*. But as far as influence upon Universal's film are concerned, the most relevant of Haggard's works is *She: A History of Adventure*, which was serialised from 1886 to 1887. *The Mummy*'s screenwriter John L. Balderston was most definitely familiar with *She*, as he was writing a script for a film adaptation of the novel at the same time that he was working on *The Mummy*.[12]

The backstory to *She* involves an ancient Egyptian priest of Isis named Kallikrates, who forsook his vows and fled Egypt with his lover, the princess Amenartas. The couple reached the land of Kor, ruled over by an Arab queen named Ayesha; this queen fell in love with Kallikrates, but the priest remained faithful to Amenartas. The main body of the novel follows a modern expedition to the fabled Kor, one member of which – Leo Vincey – is an identical descendant of Kallikrates. The travellers find the land still ruled by Ayesha, who has prolonged her existence using a mysterious fire. She declares that Leo is Kallikrates reincarnated, and tries once more to take him as her love. She finally attempts a ritual that will leave him as ageless as she is; but the ritual backfires and causes Ayesha to age rapidly before dying.

While the character roles were juggled around somewhat and the lost civilisation element removed, much of this narrative is clearly visible in *The Mummy*. Some of the smaller details of the two stories overlap as well: Ayesha has the ability to call forth images in a pool of water and can also strike her enemies dead with an invisible force, two powers possessed by Imhotep.

Furthermore, mummies are a recurring motif in *She*. The people of Kor are established to have mummified their dead, with the narrator finding the perfectly-preserved foot of an ancient woman in a decidedly Gautier-esque sequence ('Poor little foot! I set it down upon the stone bench where it had lain for so many thousand years, and wondered whose was the beauty that it had upborne through the pomp and pageantry of a forgotten civilisation'). Ayesha herself initially appears as a 'swathed mummy-like form', and her choice of attire later causes an observer to mistake her for a walking corpse. As she withers and dies, she is reduced to something resembling 'a badly-preserved Egyptian mummy'.

Most striking of all, Ayesha uses her magic to partially revive the mummified body of Kallikrates. As the corpse lies on the ground beneath a sheet, the narrator witnesses the body apparently quivering and the sheet moving as though the person below was breathing in sleep. Ayesha then halts her magic: 'Of what good is it to recall the semblance of life when I cannot recall the spirit?' she asks. 'Even if thou stoodest before me thou wouldst not know me, and couldst but do what I bid thee. The life in thee would be *my* life, and not *thy* life, Kallikrates.' This scene has a very close parallel in the climax to *The Mummy*, when Imhotep declares that he could revive Anck-es-en-Amons mummy' – but 'it would be a mere thing that moved at my will, without a soul'. Both Ayesha and Imhotep ultimately destroy the body of their respective lover, to demonstrate that the individual's soul now exists elsewhere.

Between them, these three works – Arthur Conan Doyle's 'The Ring of Thoth', Bram Stoker's *The Jewel of Seven Stars*, H. Rider Haggard's *She* – include almost all of the key ingredients to the plot of *The Mummy*. But not all of these ingredients were in place when the film's script began development. The next chapter of this book will look at how *The Mummy* took shape at Universal, and the significant transformations that it underwent along the way.

FOOTNOTES

4. Leca, A-P. *The Cult of the Immortal: Mummies and the Ancient Way of Death* (Granada, St Albans, 1983) pp218-9

5. Pringle, H., *The Mummy Congress: Science, Obsession, and the Everlasting Dead* (Hyperion Books, New York, 2001) p207
6. Day, J., *The Mummy's Curse: Mummymania in the English-Speaking World* (Routledge, Abingdon, Oxon, 2006) p25
7. In act 4, scene 1 of Macbeth, the ingredients in the cauldron include '[w]itches' mummy' alongside the better-known eye of newt and toe of frog. In *Vathek* the titular Caliph ritually burns various objects as an offering to infernal powers; amongst these are 'mummies that had been brought from the catacombs of the ancient Pharaohs'. The evil spirit on the receiving end of this offer informs Vathek that 'my nostrils have been regaled by the savour of thy mummies'.
8. For further analysis, see Chambers, S. J., 'The Corpse of the Future: Jane C. Loudon's *The Mummy!* and Victorian Science Fiction', *ClarkesworldMagazine.com*, http://clarkesworldmagazine.com/chambers_12_12/
9. Leca, A-P. *The Cult of the Immortal: Mummies and the Ancient Way of Death* (Granada, St Albans, 1983) pp219-20
10. Tyson, D., *The Dream World of H. P. Lovecraft: His Life, His Demons, His Universe* (Llewellyn Publications, Woodbury, 2010) p78
11. Shaw, I. and Nicholson, P., *British Museum Dictionary of Ancient Egypt* (BCA, London, 1995) p120
12. Rigby, J., *American Gothic: Six Decades of Classic American Horror Cinema* (Signum Books, Cambridge, 2017) p127

Chapter 2. From Cagliostro to Imhotep: The Writing Process

When Howard Carter discovered Tutankhamun's tomb in November 1922, he started a wave of cultural enthusiasm for all things ancient Egyptian.[13] This was a long-lasting phenomenon: the tomb was largely intact when the resting places of so many other pharaohs had long since been plundered, and the treasures within were so plentiful that it was nearly a decade before the final shipment of artefacts reached the Egyptian Museum in Cairo.[14] The ancient art of Egypt was back in the sun, and the modern entertainment industry realised that it had some catching up to do. The influence of Tutankhamun spread across artists, novelists, playwrights, singers – and film studios.

'Tutmania' had peaked by the start of the 1930s, but it was sufficiently fresh in the public mind for Universal's head of production Carl Laemmle Jr. to sense a commercial opportunity. And so, in early 1932 Laemmle decided that Universal's next horror film would have an Egyptian theme. The first requirement was to produce a plot, and Laemmle handed this assignment to a pair of writers: Universal scenario department head Richard Schayer, and established novelist Nina Wilcox Putnam. They responded with a nine-page synopsis entitled *Cagliostro*.[15]

Considering the impetus behind the project, and the form that the film eventually took, it may come as a surprise that the synopsis took its name not from an ancient Egyptian figure but from a personage of eighteenth-century Europe. Born Giuseppe Balsamo in 1743,[16] Count Cagliostro (as he styled himself) was an alleged mystic who became a prominent society man through his occult theatrics. His contemporary Giacomo Casanova dismissed him as 'a trickster and a clown [whose] manners were no better than his pedigree', although nineteenth-century occultist Helena Blavatsky was more sympathetic: 'His fate was that of every human being who shows that he knows more than other people. He was "stoned to death" by persecutions, lies [and] defamatory accusations'.[17]

Cagliostro claimed that, while visiting the pyramids, he 'came to know the mysteries of the different temples, which are forbidden to ordinary mortals'. A freemason, he published a pamphlet entitled *Rituel de la Maçonnerie égyptienne* (*Ritual of Egyptian*

Freemasonry) which added an Egyptian veneer to what was in large part Judeo-Christian mysticism, with the text identifying Cagliostro himself as the 'Great Copt'. Egyptian Freemasonry consisted of various rites, from the calling of spirits into a crystal ball 'according to Grecio-Egyptian necromancy' to an elaborate – and medically questionable – dietary regime centred on mysterious substances prepared by Cagliostro. The latter process allegedly had a rejuvenating effect on the subject: 'his body will become as pure as an innocent boy's,' claimed the pamphlet.[18]

This is likely why Cagliostro became associated with one of the holy grails of alchemy: the elixir of eternal life. An anonymous 1835 text entitled *Thaumaturgia, Or, Elucidations of the Marvellous* contains an account of how Cagliostro sold an everyday stomach medicine 'under a most exorbitant price', claiming that it was an elixir that had granted him more than two hundred years of life.[19]

The larger-than-life figure of Cagliostro was irresistible to authors of romance. Alexander Dumas wrote a novel, *Joseph Balsamo* (serialised 1846-49), in which Cagliostro is depicted as using his mystical wiles to influence the French court. This fictional Cagliostro boasts of having an elixir of eternal life – although instead of granting literal immortality, it has purportedly opened up memories of his past incarnations and granted him the wisdom of centuries' lived experience. In Dumas' 1849-50 sequel *The Queen's Necklace* (*Le Collier de la reine*) Cagliostro claims to have lived for three thousand years, making him a survivor of the ancient world.

It is this fanciful notion of Cagliostro as a millennia-old magician that formed the core of Putnam and Schayer's synopsis, with a dash of fashionable Egyptology thrown on top for good measure.

The synopsis[20] opens with a locked-room mystery in which millionaire H.C.H. Whemple is found inexplicably dead. The hero is a young doctor named Jack Foster, who pursues a relationship with cinema ticket-seller Helen Dorrington. Helen receives word that a long-lost uncle from Australia has moved into H.C.H. Whemple's mansion; when she visits him he turns out to be blind, and living alone with a black servant (referred to as a 'giant Nubian'). Helen suggests that Dr. Jack could cure his blindness, but the uncle refuses to allow Jack into the mansion, losing his temper when he learns that Helen and Jack are romantically attached to one another.

Meanwhile, San Francisco is hit by a spate of mysterious crimes. A bank vault is found to have been robbed without sign of breaking and entry, the guards having suddenly died of heart disease. Witnesses describe seeing the shadow of a large black man at the scene of the crime.

Professor Thernley Whemple, archaeologist brother of the dead millionaire, encounters Helen's uncle and notes that he has a remarkable resemblance to the historical Cagliostro. The synopsis offers a potted account of this personage, but the key point is entirely fictional: according to Whemple, the immortal Cagliostro was betrayed by a beautiful woman, and spent the following centuries finding and murdering women who resembled his lost love. As the uncle was previously seen holding an ancient Egyptian portrait of a woman resembling Helen, the audience would at this point have realised the truth: the 'uncle' is in fact Cagliostro, and Helen – the image of the woman who spurned him – is his next victim.

Dr. Jack expresses scepticism about the possibility of eternal life, but Whemple insists that there is archaeological evidence of such a thing being known to the ancient Egyptians, also citing the legendary figures of Merlin and the Wandering Jew. Helen then calls Jack with a chilling anecdote: she woke up in the night to see her uncle by her bed, surrounded by a weird light. She grabbed a nearby crucifix and turned on the light to find her uncle gone, leaving only a pair of dusty hand-prints.

Cagliostro then has his servant kidnap Helen and trap her in a cell. The evil genius is able to watch her plight 'through the medium of his television-machine'. The servant also robs the home of Thernley Whemple, stealing articles that relate to Cagliostro's true identity.

The police investigating the crimes come to suspect the black servant, who matches witness descriptions, but he is able to prove that he did not leave the mansion at the time of the incidents. In fact, '[h]is shadow has of course left it, projected by television, in an effort to mislead the police.' The police do manage to locate a low-level accomplice to the crimes, and persuade him to act as a stool pigeon on the next robbery – an attempt to steal condensed nitrates and other chemicals from a vault.

Professor Whemple, a police contact, hears of this plan. As the robbery is taking place, Whemple breaks into his dead brother's mansion through a secret entrance and finds a set of syringes alongside what he recognises as part of the immortality formula, which he confiscates. He also sees Cagliostro commanding the robbery over a radio; at the horrifying sight of the villain killing people with a 'death-ray,' Whemple makes a sound. Cagliostro – who was merely pretending to be blind – discovers Whemple's presence and has him thrown into a cell adjacent to Helen's prison.

The police learn of Whemple and Helen's disappearances; with the aid of Dr. Jack, they storm Cagliostro's mansion. The servant holds the attackers at bay for a while, but having lost his life-giving formula Cagliostro begins to decay. By the time the police rescue the two captives, all they find of Cagliostro are his clothing and a few handfuls of 'the sort of dust to which Egyptian mummies crumble when exposed to the air'.

This version of the story has little in common with the finished film. The characters are largely recognisable, but this is because they are stereotypes: the young hero, the sinister villain, the damsel-in-distress, the brutish henchman and the all-knowing professor. The one significant incident that survived into *The Mummy* intact occurs when Helen visits Cagliostro for the first time; her dog reacts with hostility, and Cagliostro has the animal sent outside where it falls victim to his death ray. This sequence of events is played out in *The Mummy* when Helen visits Imhotep at his lair accompanied by her dog.

The presence of the television-machine, death-ray and nitrate formula suggests that *Cagliostro* was inspired by pulp science fiction rather than supernatural fantasy. The narrative penned by Putnam and Schayer reads like something straight out of *Amazing Stories*, the pioneering science fiction magazine founded by Hugo Gernsback in 1926.[21] This publication found fertile material in stories of disintegration rays (Philip Francis Nowlan's 'Armageddon 2419 A.D.'), televisual devices ('Treasures of Tantalus' by Garrett Smith) and larger-than-life criminals itching to put such wondrous inventions to bad use (Garrett P. Serviss' 'The Moon Metal').[22] *Amazing Stories* grew out of Gernsback's earlier radio magazines, which sometimes printed science fiction; this cultural backdrop can be glimpsed in the *Cagliostro* synopsis, as hero Dr. Jack is identified as 'a radio fan, and an expert radio-man'. Other elements of the narrative – the emphasis on police procedure, a character acting as stool pigeon, a discussion about alibis – show that the story also has a foot in the crime genre.

Another relevant comparison point is Sax Rohmer's Fu Manchu series, which began in

1912 and had been adapted for the screen multiple times since the silent era.[23] Across his appearances in print and film, the Chinese crimelord Fu Manchu mixed science fiction gadgetry with exotic supernaturalism. For example, Boris Karloff's *The Mask of Fu Manchu* has the villain invoke the ghost of Genghis Khan while also operating a laboratory filled with electrical apparatus, including a gun-like device that shoots deadly arcs.

The set of genre elements found in the *Cagliostro* synopsis did turn eventually up in a Universal film – just not in *The Mummy*. *Cagliostro* has definite similarities to *The Invisible Ray*, released in 1936; here, Boris Karloff plays an astronomer suffering from a weird radiation poisoning that requires regular doses of an antidote. After killing a few people with a death-ray, Karloff loses his antidote and ends up dissolving.

Despite its glaring differences from the finished product, the synopsis plants the seed for what would become *The Mummy* by hinting that Cagliostro is some sort of animated mummy, or at least, that his immortal status has given him mummy-like attributes as a side effect. Throughout the story he is associated with dust: Helen notices strange dust in his mansion, he leaves dusty handprints on her bed (not unlike the handprint left by Imhotep in the prologue of the finished film) and finally crumbles into a pile of dust – which the treatment explicitly compares to that of a crumbled Egyptian mummy.

THE SCRIPT TAKES SHAPE

When Nina Wilcox Putnam fleshed the synopsis into a full screenplay, dated February 1932, the story moved away from science fiction and towards the occult and supernatural. Doubts about the title had already set in at Universal, and so this draft of the script bears the header *Cagliostro, or The King of the Dead*.

In this version H.C.H. Whemple has become Professor Joseph Whemple, curator of the Egyptian department at a New York museum. The film begins with Whemple meeting a strange individual in the museum: 'a tall, lean man whose cadaverous face is shadowed by a wide brimmed black hat' and who is equipped with a long cloak and a cane like that of Osiris. After drawing attention to a fake included in the museum's collection, the man introduces himself as Dr. Astro. 'You are the chap who can read the future and whom the big Wall Street men are all consulting these days' replies Whemple.

Dr. Astro then notices the mummy case of one Princess Iris. A flashback shows the burial of this personage, observed by Dr. Astro – who is, of course, the immortal Cagliostro. He weeps over the body of Iris; back in the present day he is still poring over her sarcophagus. Whemple disturbs him and he departs, leaving dusty hand-prints on both the sarcophagus and one of Whemple's books.

Joseph Whemple later holds a gathering at his house, introducing characters familiar from the earlier draft of the story. Dr. Jack Foster is there; Thernley Whemple, now Henry Whemple, is also present, as is Jack's lover Helen, who now has the surname Barostzi and works as the professor's secretary. The dialogue reveals that Helen is the daughter of an American mother and an Egyptian father, and harbours a great interest in Egypt's ancient history. The guest of honour is Dr. Astro – who departs the group early, handing Joseph Whemple a charm in the shape of Osiris as a parting gift.

Astro returns to his hotel room, which is home to 'a large and elaborate television-radio machine' and 'a giant Nubian, dressed in Egyptian dragoman costume'; the latter is identified by the script as being 'the magician's slave in spirit if not in fact'. Operating the television machine, Astro obtains an image of Professor Whemple alone at home; he then wheels out another device, 'a death ray machine which sputters and gives off blue sparks'. Focusing the death ray on the television, Astro causes the professor to die from heart failure.

The police investigating the death speak to the surviving Whemple brother, who lets slip a curious fact about the deceased: 'my brother grew to be afraid of the mummies in his department... [he] actually believed the things might come to life.' Meanwhile, the coroner notices a strange star-like burn on the victim's chest.

Back at his hotel room, Dr. Astro is undergoing the treatment that extends his life. This turns out to be more complicated than a mere jab with a syringe, and involves him being transformed into a bandaged mummy:

> Nubian lifts off cover and we see the mummy in its stained bindings. It looks as if it had not been disturbed for a thousand years. It writhes slowly. The Nubian... starts unwinding the wrappings skilfully and swiftly.

A frightful sight lies beneath those bandages:

> Then, suddenly, the corpse sits bolt upright in the mummy case. It is naked to the waist, showing a terrible scar where the body was once slit open to remove the intestines. It is a gaunt, thin body, and the flesh is grey-brown and parchment-like, the eyes mere sunken pits of darkness. The erect body slowly takes on human semblance as the air strikes it and the gruesome figure becomes Dr. Astro. Through all this, we hear the subdued whimpering and muttering of the terrified Nubian.

Astro rejuvenates himself in time to meet Henry Whemple, who names him the new curator at the museum. Astro then hires Helen as his secretary, recognising her as the reincarnation of Princess Isis. Helen visits Astro in what was once Joseph Whemple's mansion, now transformed into what the script identifies as 'a deliberate piece of good hokum frankly designed to impress the public… typical of the reception rooms of charlatans since time immemorial'.

Astro reacts badly to the sight of Helen's dog. He gives her an Osiris charm to attach to the dog's collar, and after she has retreated to her sleeping quarters, Astro kills the dog with his death ray. In the morning, Helen dons an ancient Egyptian costume given to her by the servant. Astro uses a 'hypnotic gaze' in an attempt to recover her memories of her past life, but desists when she shows discomfort.

Dr. Jack comes to visit Helen, and after gushing over Astro's scientific prowess ('He's three jumps ahead of Edison') she shows her new boss's laboratory to Jack. But when Jack tries to embrace his fiancée she 'eludes him, not unkindly but coolly rather than coyly', indicating that Astro has turned their relationship into a love triangle. However, she insists that she is not attracted to Astro, stating that she views him as a sort of uncle. 'These damned Egyptians used to marry their sisters,' quips Jack; 'being your uncle wouldn't stop him.' This comment goes down badly with Helen – who, after all, is half Egyptian.

Alone together, Helen and Astro examine the Egyptian Book of the Dead, with a particular excerpt being highlighted: 'To go in and out of my grave – to cool myself in its shadow. Even as Osiris is not destroyed, so shall I not be destroyed.' Astro explains the workings of eternal life to Helen:

My child, you must first clear your mind of the thought of mummifying as an end in itself. What I am trying to explain to you is that suspended animation was practiced by the Rosicrucians as early as the building of the Temple of the Twelve Cells.

Helen picks up a document containing Plutarch's account of the Osiris/Isis myth. 'Plutarch says the Ka, or animation, shall re-enter the body at intervals – Do you really believe that?' she asks. 'Yes,' replies Astro, 'and furthermore the soul can be transferred from one body to another.'

Meanwhile, Dr. Jack speaks with Whemple. Jack expresses fear that Astro is 'trying some of his damned tricks' on Helen and asks Whemple to expose him as a fraud. Whemple responds by showing a portrait of Cagliostro ('who is supposed to be no less a person than Osiris himself') and offers the theory that this eighteenth-century mystic is alive and well in the guise of Dr. Astro. Jack is sceptical, but Whemple tells him about the legend of the Wandering Jew and the allegedly immortal Count St. Germain (this sequence is retained in large part from the original synopsis.)

The two men decide to hold a séance attended by 'the finest minds in the country' and invite Astro to come along in the hopes of exposing him. The séance takes place in Whemple's home; the guests include 'members of the Society of Psychic Research, noted doctors, a few statesmen, a famous preacher or two, a Catholic priest and a Rabbi… an audience well calculated to strike terror to the heart of any faker'.

There, Astro apparently reads the mind of one of the men trying to test him. He then turns his powers on Jack. 'You think I am dangerous. You believe I am a criminal, not a scientist, and that I intend harm to someone dear to you… but any harm to this person is the furthest thing from my mind… it is unwise to make enemies of those the gods love, because the gods can also destroy.'

Next, Astro performs 'one of the most famous of the Indian Fakir tricks' ('[Nina Wilcox Putnam] is familiar with this trick having seen it in India and possessing 44 consecutive photographs of the trick,' notes the script). This entails planting a mango seed in a pot of soil and making it instantaneously sprout into a tree. Afterwards, Helen enters the room and Astro causes her to levitate. The audience, initially sceptical, is awed.

A doctor in the room asks if Astro can raise the dead. Astro responds by lifting the hood of his cloak ('his figure suggests the conventional pictures of Death') and calling forth spirits. The ghost of Joseph Whemple appears in the room in an effect that would have been achieved through double exposure. Jack asks the deceased man who murdered him; but before the spirit can reply, Astro suddenly overturns the table and shuts off the light. When the light returns, the ghost has gone.

After the séance, Helen speaks to Jack and reaffirms how much she admires Astro. But she also notes that some things about him bother her – such as his habit of leaving dusty prints wherever he places his hands. While visiting Helen, Jack sees the collar of her dead dog, and pockets the Osiris charm attached to it. Astro walks in, greeting Helen as 'my dear niece,' and Jack departs.

Astro has the mummy of Princess Iris transported to his home, ostensibly so that he can conduct repairs on it in his laboratory. He then goes to Helen and pressures her to take part in an occult experiment. Although she tries to drop out, Astro places her under hypnotic control: 'You will consent. You are going to obey. The soul will depart and the soul of Iris will take its place. Is it not so?'

Moving like a sleepwalker, Helen undergoes a process that involves being injected in the arm with an unspecified substance. The Nubian servant warns Astro that 'the hour is approaching when the master must again join the dead for a little while,' but the magician insists that he will be finished in time.

Having learned that Jack has taken the charm from the dog's collar, Astro heads to his television-machine. He obtains a picture of Jack at home and blasts him with the death ray, apparently killing him. However, Jack has by this point disposed of the Osiris charm; as a result the ray missed its mark, hurting Jack but not killing him.

Astro and his Nubian servant then begin a ritual which the script cites as having been lifted from Adolph Erman's *Handbook of Egyptian Religion*. The two break open the seal to a shrine containing a statue of the god Amon-Ra and kill a goat in sacrifice; the script has the Nubian holding the animal's severed head as the blood drips out, a remarkably graphic image for a film of this era.

Ghostly priests of ancient Egypt appear and join in the ritual. Next, the gods themselves manifest as Astro invokes them one by one: Anubis, Wepwawet, Sokaris, Sekhmet,

Set, Horus, Bast, Isis, Hathor. The script suggests that 'interesting creatures of Egyptian mythology' such as serpents, vampire bats and human-headed birds could also manifest. Finally, the statue of Amon-Ra comes to life, dominating the scene as the mummy of Iris is consumed by flames. The ritual results in Helen recovering her senses, now with the mind of Iris. 'Beloved,' she says to Astro. 'I had such a strange dream. I thought that I had died.'

Astro explains to his love that it has been three thousand years since she last walked the earth. 'I have found the secret of eternal life,' he says; 'of how to keep my limbs together, the brain within my skull where should be only dust and barren bone.'

Back at his home, Jack recovers from the blast given to him by the misfiring death ray. He retrieves the discarded Osiris charm and breaks it open to expose a wire coil, used in targeting the ray. Realising that Helen is in danger, he sets off to fetch help.

Meanwhile, Astro explains the means of his immortality to Helen/Iris: 'Once every three moons I must be as the dead... In my shroudings I must lie until new strength is sucked into my dry and brittle flesh. Then, I come forth again to live anew.' This process involves a twelve-day sojourn in the underworld, and Helen/Iris is horrified to learn that he expects her to undergo the same treatment: 'Iris! Hear me. You shall be made even as I... a mummified thing that yet lives.'

'No, I tell thee! No!' replies the woman. 'I love this beautiful young body too well, I will not die again!' Astro tries to hypnotise her; but as he is starting to decay once more, his powers fail him. Helen runs far enough away to see the Nubian alongside an Egyptian embalming table, complete with all the requisite tools. 'Ha! Ha! See – we are well prepared for you,' gloats Astro.

But the Nubian cannot bring himself to harm her. 'May the curse of Amen [sic] rest upon you,' barks Astro, the only point at which the theme of curses is mentioned in the script. Then Jack arrives at the building accompanied by police; the sound of his voice breaks Astro's spell over Helen, and she regains her mind. The treacherous Nubian leads the police to the quarters of his master, and they arrive in time to 'watch Astro decay by the same method of stop shots which was used in *Dr. Jekyll and Mr. Hyde*'. When all that is left of Cagliostro is a pile of dust, Jack embraces Helen.

A Transitional Stage

Much of *The Mummy* is recognisable in *Cagliostro, or The King of the Dead*, although the events do not necessarily occur in the same order.

Some sequences make more sense in this draft than they do in the final film. The death of Helen's dog is a curiously out-of-place incident in *The Mummy*, as the dog is never mentioned before and its demise has no impact on the plot. In the earlier script, on the other hand, the collar of the dead dog is a Chekhov's gun that impacts Cagliostro's attempt to kill Jack later on. The threatened fate of Helen during the climax is also more coherent: *The Mummy* never clarifies why Helen needs to be embalmed before becoming immortal, but *Cagliostro, or The King of the Dead* establishes that Cagliostro's immortality involves him periodically becoming a shrivelled mummy, and that Helen would have to undergo the same process.

Other aspects of the script were tidied up in *The Mummy*. The scene where Cagliostro summons the animal-headed gods of Egypt would have offered much spectacle, but the deities actually achieve very little: all the ritual does is partially restore the memories of Princess Iris, something quickly undone. Cagliostro's death, meanwhile, seems an anti-climax; the earlier synopsis had Whemple condemn him by confiscating his formula, but there is no such incident in this draft, with Cagliostro instead dying more or less due to mere distraction on his part. *The Mummy* ties the two loose ends together by having Imhotep struck down by a manifestation of the goddess Isis.

Also noticeable are a few out-of-place fragments from the earlier *Cagliostro* synopsis, such as an aimless subplot involving the murdered man's inheritance and greater involvement from the police. Although this version of the story dispenses with Cagliostro masquerading as Helen's uncle, the dialogue retains traces of this concept: Helen states that she sees Dr. Astro as an uncle; Jack later refers to Astro as 'Helen's so-called uncle'; and in another scene, Astro identifies Helen as his niece.

The characters continue to take shape, although they still had a number of revisions to go before appearing onscreen. The script has the Whemples as Americans, rather than Englishmen as they are in the film. The family also has a different structure: in the finished film Dr. Jack becomes Joseph Whemple's archaeologist son Frank, while Henry Whemple loses his family connections and becomes Dr. Muller. The heroine in *Cagliostro, or The King of the Dead* is the American-Egyptian secretary Helen Barostzi; in *The Mummy* she is the half-Egyptian daughter of a British governor, and is granted the appropriately Anglo-Norman surname of Grosvenor.

But the biggest changes relate to the villain of the story. The original synopsis has the mad scientist Calgiostro; the final film has the undead, fez-wearing magician Ardath Bey; but the *Cagliostro, or The King of the Dead* script features a curious half-way point between the two. Dr. Astro still has his television and death-ray, but the script generally plays him up as a magician rather than a mad scientist. And yet, his magical trappings are still rather different from those of Karloff's character in the finished film.

The script makes repeated references to figures from European occult tradition: Dr. Astro is said to be familiar with the methods of Gassner, Casanova, Madame Blavatsky and 'Messer' (presumably a mistyped reference to Franz Mesmer, after whom mesmerism is named) while Whemple compares him to Count St. Germaine and the medieval legend of the Wandering Jew. Where Ardath Bey wears a scarab beetle ring, Dr. Astro prefers to adorn himself with a Rosicrucian cross. The séance scene, which has no counterpart in *The Mummy*, is based mainly on the workings of Western spiritualists, albeit with an Indian fakir trick incorporated. Dr. Astro also has ties to American stage illusionists: he claims to have counted Harry Houdini and Howard Thurston amongst his pupils, although he taught them no more than 'childish tricks'.

The script's conception of magic, then, comes ultimately from a combination of European occultism and American stage conjuring. Each of those traditions appropriated the trappings of ancient Egyptian religion to provide exotic backdrops, and *Cagliostro, or The King of the Dead* does the same, particularly during the climactic parade of Egyptian deities.

Finally, the medical procedure of Cagliostro injecting himself with a nitrate solution, as described in the synopsis, is no more. The script has the bizarre scene of Dr. Astro being temporarily transformed into a mummy in what is clearly an early version of *The Mummy*'s iconic prologue.

THE BIRTH OF *THE MUMMY*

In the summer of 1932 John L. Balderston joined the project and provided script rewrites. Balderston re-worked the villain's backstory, doing away with all traces of his earlier interpretations as mad scientist and stage conjurer and changing him from the immortal Cagliostro to the resurrected Im-Ho-Tep (the hyphens can be found in the shooting script, but were removed by the time the film's credits were added).[24]

As is frequently the case, the narrative in the shooting script is not identical to that of the finished film.[25] Director Karl Freund re-ordered certain portions of the script for better dramatic effect, and removed a number of scenes and dialogue exchanges altogether. For one, the script has a poignant scene where Ardath Bey presents Helen with the jewellery of Anck-es-en-Amon, stirring long-dormant memories; it also has more material dealing with the deadly rivalry between Helen's dog (that hardy survivor from the earliest synopsis) and Ardath Bey's cat familiar.

Freund's most significant – and most famous – deletion is a scene revealing Helen's previous incarnations. This would have occurred after Ardath Bey and Helen arrive at the museum for the climax, taking the place of the spectacle in the *Cagliostro* script where Dr. Astro summons a procession of gods. As scripted, the scene has Ardath Bey use a mirror to conjure up images of Helen's past lives: the audience was to have seen Zita Johann playing, in turn, an eighteenth-century French lady in a powdered wig; a medieval damsel bidding farewell to crusading knights; a Saxon princess committing suicide to escape Viking raiders; and a Christian martyr being thrown to lions in ancient Rome.

This sequence was filmed in its entirety. A few stills exist showing Helen's alter egos; one of the characters she was to have encountered – a Saxon warrior played by Henry Victor – is actually listed in the credits to the film; and part of the final segment, showing Imhotep being buried alive, was ultimately used as the conclusion to the earlier ancient Egyptian sequence. However, the majority of the reincarnation sequence was left on the cutting room floor, presumably to avoid slowing the pace of the climax. The flashback would also have created something of a plot hole: since Helen is implied to have inherited the soul of Anck-es-en-Amon from the ancestry of her Egyptian mother, how could it have passed through the bodies of all these European women?

Despite these last-minute changes, the story was in place with Balderston's shooting script. All it needed was a title. *Cagliostro* obviously had to go, and *The King of the Dead* did not find favour at Universal. The project at one point bore the name *Im-Ho-Tep*, but eventually, Universal settled upon a name evocative enough to launch a cinematic subgenre: *The Mummy*.[26]

Footnotes

13. For a detailed overview of this topic, see Coniam, M., *Egyptomania Goes to the Movies: From Archaeology to Popular Craze to Hollywood Fantasy* (McFarland & Company, Jefferson, 2017)
14. Allen, S. J., *Tutankhamun's Tomb: The Thrill of Discovery* (Metropolitan Museum of Art, New York, 2006) p90
15. Weaver, T. Brunas, M., and Brunas, J., *Universal Horrors: The Studio's Classic Films, 1931–1946* (McFarland, Jefferson, 2007) p64
16. Sorensen, D. R., in *The Carlyle Encyclopedia* (Fairleigh Dickinson University Press, Madison, 2004) pp61-2
17. Gervaso, R. *Cagliostro: A Biography* (Victor Gollancz Limited, London, 1974) pp242-6
18. Gervaso, R. *Cagliostro: A Biography* (Victor Gollancz Limited, London, 1974) pp70-6
19. 'An Oxonian', 'Thaumaturgia', *Archive.org*, http://archive.org/stream thaumaturgia10088gut/10088.txt
20. The *Cagliostro* synopsis and script discussed in this chapter are reproduced together in Riley, P. J., *Cagliostro, The King of the Dead: An Alternate History for Classic Film Monsters* (BearManor Media, Albany, 2010).
21. Ashley, M., *The History of the Science Fiction Magazine, Part One: 1926-1935* (New English Library, London, 1974) pp21-4
22. These works of fiction were printed in, respectively, *Amazing Stories* vol 3, no 5 (August 1928); vol 2, nos 7-8 (October-November 1927) and vol 1, no 4 (July 1926).
23. Knapp, L., 'The Movies of Fu Manchu: Part One: Harry Agar Lyons and Warner Oland', PhilSP. com, http://philsp.com/SaxRohmer/movies1.htm
24. Weaver, T. Brunas, M., and Brunas, J., *Universal Horrors: The Studio's Classic Films, 1931–1946* (McFarland, Jefferson, 2007) p64
25. The shooting script is reprinted in Riley, P. J. (ed.) *The Mummy* (MagicImage Filmbooks, Absecon, 1989).
26. Weaver, T. Brunas, M., and Brunas, J., *Universal Horrors: The Studio's Classic Films, 1931–1946* (McFarland, Jefferson, 2007) p64.

Chapter 3. The Makers of *The Mummy*

It goes without saying that *The Mummy*'s scriptwriting process represents only one strain of creative influence that went into the film. A full analysis will need to take into account not only writing but also the visual fields of direction, performances and effects. These areas were handled by both experienced stalwarts and new talents.

Karl Freund, the Director

Born in Bohemia before moving to Berlin in 1901, Karl Freund cut his teeth as a cinematographer on Weimar-era silent films. Pictures he worked on during this period include *Der Januskopf* (a now-lost 1920 version of *Dr. Jekyll and Mr. Hyde*), *The Golem* (*Der Golem*, 1920), *Metropolis* (1927) and the documentary *Berlin: Symphony of a Great City* (*Die Sinfonie der Großstadt*, 1927). Perhaps Freund's greatest achievement as cinematographer was in shooting F. W. Murnau's *The Last Laugh* (*Der letzte Mann*, 1924), a dialogue-free film where inventive camera techniques portray both the failing eyesight and the fantastic dreams of its protagonist. Freund stepped up from cinematographer to director with *Der tote Gast* (1921).

The fantasy cinema of Weimar Germany was a considerable influence upon Universal's horror output, and Freund was a linking factor between the two: after moving to America in 1929 he was hired by Universal as a cinematographer.[27] He worked in this role on *Dracula*, and there is evidence that, to a considerable extent, he actually filled in for nominal director Tod Browning. 'Tod Browning was always off to the side somewhere', recalls David Manners, who co-starred in *Dracula*. 'I remember being directed by Karl Freund, the photographer who came from Germany and had a great sense for film. I believe that he is the one who is mainly responsible for *Dracula* being watchable today.'[28] Freund went on to work as cinematographer on Universal's next Lugosi vehicle, *Murders in the Rue Morgue*, before taking the director's chair – officially, this time – with *The Mummy*.

To fully appreciate Freund's directorial approach to *The Mummy* it is best to compare the film to *Dracula*. *Dracula* is, for the most part, a visually static piece of work; only during the early sequence set in Transylvania does it capture some of the flair and atmosphere of silent German fantasy cinema. But with Freund granted full directorial control for *The Mummy*, this spirit was allowed to permeate the entire film. Freund's approach to the fantastic is subtle and understated; nowhere is this clearer than in the iconic prologue, where the mummy is largely out-of-shot following the initial close-ups of its opening eyes and languid arm movements. Many filmmakers would have shown the mummy's actions directly, but Freund understood that powerful images could be created through restraint, allowing the viewer's imagination to fill in the details.

JOHN L. BALDERSTON, THE WRITER

While it was Richard Schayer and Nina Wilcox Putnam who laid out the earliest version of *The Mummy*'s storyline, it was John L. Balderston who reworked it from a muddled mixture of magic and mad science to a narrative that defined a subgenre. It was also Balderston who provided the dialogue, which ranges from the portentous intonations of Muller, to the romantic banter between Frank and Helen, to the poetic proclamations of Ardath Bey – complete with the occasional foray into iambic pentameter ('…since we loved in Thebes of old…').

In terms of experience, Balderston was the perfect man for the job. He had been involved with two of Universal's previous horror hits: Balderston's stage version of *Dracula* (rewritten from Hamilton Dean's script) served as the basis for the 1931 film version, and he was one of multiple writers responsible for bringing *Frankenstein* to the screen. Furthermore, in his capacity as reporter for the New York *World* he had personally observed the disinterment of Tutankhamun and delivered a vivid report of the mummy's condition: 'Embalming fluid had so soaked through the bandages that it caused them to adhere to the body, and they have to be cut away in chunks, an operation of supreme delicacy if injury to the flesh is to be avoided.'[29]

Yet Balderston is also the likely culprit for one of the film's most heavily-criticised aspects: its close similarity to *Dracula*. Nina Wilcox Putnam's *Cagliostro* storyline bore no significant resemblance to *Dracula* beyond what would reasonably be expected from two films belonging to the same genre, so *The Mummy*'s re-use of elements from the earlier film can be safely attributed to Balderston.

One glaring example of the overlap is that each film has a scene where the central characters, including the villain, are gathered in a drawing-room – with remarkably similar exchanges ensuing. The resident occult expert (in each case played by Edward Van Sloan) dotes over the heroine, who has started to fall under the villain's sway. When the villain arrives, presenting as a mortal man, the Van Sloan character unmasks him as the living dead. *Dracula*'s Van Helsing does so by showing the vampire a mirror, revealing that he has no reflection; Muller shows Ardath Bey a photo of Imhotep's mummy, revealing perhaps a little too much of a reflection.

The Mummy shares a number of its key fantasy concepts with *Dracula*, as will be discussed later in this book, and even the characters' dialogue resonates across the two films. 'She will live through the centuries to come, as I have lived,' says Count Dracula, while Ardath Bey bids Helen to 'rise again even as I have risen'.

It would be unfair to accuse Balderston of merely recycling his own writing, however. After all, his version of the *Dracula* script was itself rewritten by multiple hands before being shot.[30] With *The Mummy*, Balderston appears to have been reworking the contributions of those writers just as they had reworked his own script.

Indeed, Balderston's writing process on *The Mummy* seems distinctly magpie-like, as he gathered together appealing elements from various sources: the Putnam script, *Dracula*, H. Rider Haggard's *She* (as noted in the first chapter, Balderston had been working on an adaptation of this novel at the time) and his personal familiarity with the Tutankhamun expedition. He reportedly disliked Hollywood, as his scripts were revised more substantially than they were in the theatre;[31] but his contributions to *The Mummy* indicate that he was able to fit neatly into Hollywood's creative environment nonetheless, borrowing and adapting the ideas of others where necessary.

There is a lingering question over Balderston's involvement with *The Mummy*, one raised by Paul M. Jensen in his DVD commentary for the film. The shooting script, credited to Balderston alone, contains detailed camera instructions which the film follows closely. Is this a sign that Balderston deserves some of the credit for the innovative cinematography that is typically attributed to Freund?

As Jensen concludes, however, it is unlikely that Balderston had much input into the film's camerawork. Freund was an experienced cinematographer, while Balderston was a playwright by trade who is not known to have had any experience with film direction. That said, film is a collaborative medium, and it is wise to avoid making too many assumptions about where the contributions of one person end and those of another begin.

BORIS KARLOFF, THE UNCANNY

That publicity for *The Mummy* referred to its star as 'Karloff the Uncanny' neatly summarises his public image at the time of release. Hot off the success of *Frankenstein* – the opening credits to which left him unnamed, giving him a veneer of mystery – Boris Karloff was established as Hollywood's biggest monster. As his career continued, he showed himself to be not only a monster, but a monster of many faces.

Born William Henry Pratt in 1887, Boris Karloff moved from his native England to Canada prior to arriving in Hollywood. His career as a film actor began in the silent era, when he was relegated largely to bit-parts. His big break did not arrive until 1931 when he was chosen by director James Whale as a replacement for Bela Lugosi in *Frankenstein*.[32] By the time he played Imhotep, Karloff had already starred in two more horror films: Universal's *The Old Dark House* and MGM's *The Mask of Fu Manchu*, both released in 1932.

Karloff's signature role as Frankenstein's Monster necessitated heavy make-up and he undertook a transformation similar to those of Lon Chaney, recently-deceased star of Universal's *The Phantom of the Opera* and *The Hunchback of Notre Dame*. But Karloff's metamorphosis was not as thorough as Chaney's more notorious face-changes. The iconic appearance of Frankenstein's Monster was based ultimately on an exaggeration of what Karloff looked like under his make-up; the only parts of the actor's distinctive visage to be obscured rather than accentuated were his penetrating eyes, which were partially concealed by false eyelids. Perhaps not coincidentally, Karloff's eyes are focal points of attention in *The Mummy*: Imhotep's powers are symbolised by lingering close-ups of his intense glare.

A major distinction between Karloff and Chaney is that, unlike his mostly silent precursor, Karloff became a star of the sound era – although his early horror roles did not always make use of his vocal skills. Karloff's characters in *Frankenstein* and *The Old Dark House* uttered only inarticulate grunts and wails. *The Mask of Fu Manchu* gave him a speaking role, but cast him unimaginatively as a gloating, cackling cliché. His character in *The Mummy* was conceived along similar lines, as the *Cagliostro* script called for Karloff to rub his hands with glee while operating his death ray, but his performance onscreen turned out to be of a very different sort. As Ardath Bey, Karloff perfected a distinctively quiet, sombre form of menace.

The melancholy tones of Boris Karloff have joined Bela Lugosi's lilting accent and Vincent Price's pantomime cadence as a voice synonymous with horror films. His intonations have been extensively imitated and parodied, most famously in Bobby Pickett's 1962 novelty hit 'Monster Mash' and the ironic opening scene to *Night of the Living Dead* (1968). *The Mummy* is the film where audiences first heard his voice used to full effect.

Although Karloff played the role of Frankenstein's Monster in *Bride of Frankenstein* (1935) and *Son of Frankenstein* (1939), he would never again play the mummy. It fell upon other actors to grind this character into a mere stereotype; Karloff's performance as Imhotep and his alter ego Ardath Bey remains a one-off, an unforgettable high point of the actor's career.

ZITA JOHANN, THE HEROINE

When writing the film's script, John L. Balderston had a specific look in mind for the reincarnated Egyptian heroine Helen Grosvenor:

> For the heroine a dark girl of Egyptian appearance is essential, she should approximate in type to the bust of Nefertiti in the Berlin Museum [the script elsewhere notes that Nefertiti was 'probably the mother of the real Anck-es-en-Amon']. Something mysterious and deep about her; an emotional actress of high caliber is needed to play the last sequence which calls for depth and power as well as subtlety.

Fig 3: Helen (Zita Johann) in Egyptian dress

While Balderston's choice for the part was Katherine Hepburn, the role ultimately went to Zita Johann. Born in Hungary, Johann had led a successful stage career in New York but was struggling to make her mark in Hollywood: her most notable film role prior to The Mummy was in The Struggle (1931), the disastrous final picture of D. W. Griffith.[33] She turned out to be a worthy addition to the Universal horror pantheon, and her role in The Mummy allowed her ample opportunity to demonstrate this.

As a character, Helen Grosvenor is more forceful than many of her counterparts in the studio's other horror films. Helen Chandler and Frances Dade's characters in Dracula gossip girlishly in their shared boudoir about the alluring visitor from Transylvania; Mae Clarke and Gloria Stuart's heroines in Frankenstein and The Invisible Man (1933) are passive characters who spend their time pining for their science-obsessed lovers. In contrast, Zita Johann's character shows clear spirit – indeed, two distinct varieties of spirit. In her modern-day guise Helen has a strain of knowing humour, as when she teases Frank after he admits to falling in love with Anck-es-en-Amon's mummy ('Do you have to open graves to find girls to fall in love with?') Upon regaining the ancient princess' psyche, she adopts an appropriate dignity and gravitas ('What mummy has usurped my eternal resting place?'). No shrieking damsel reliant on a male hero for rescue, Helen is a sacred priestess who uses her connection with a higher power to destroy Imhotep.

But despite being offered the title role in *Dracula's Daughter* (1936),[34] Zita Johann did not remain amongst Universal's horror stars. Her experience working on *The Mummy* was singularly unpleasant, and she pinned the blame on one man: director Karl Freund.[35]

According to Johann's later account of her experiences, Freund mounted a bullying campaign against her; she interpreted this as a concerted attempt to turn her into a scapegoat. 'The director, Karl Freund, really was a terrible sadist,' she said. 'This was his first directorial job – he was a cameraman – and he had to find an alibi for the front office in case he was late. So he picked me, naturally.' According to Johann, this harassment began when the two first met:

> Before shooting started, I asked Freund and his wife over for dinner. Without a hello or a name – his or mine – he said 'In von schene you haff to blay it from the vaste up NOOD!' I believe he expected me to say, 'The hell I will!' Instead I said, 'Well, it's alright with me, if you can get it past the censors.' Freund, so sure that I'd blow my top, knew that I had him.

But Freund did not let up. For the scene where Helen visits Ardath Bey wearing a tight-fitting suit, the director made Johann stand against a board for two days so as to avoid any creases in her costume. Johann was so exhausted that at one point she keeled over and remained unconscious for an hour; as the studio was in a hard-to-access location, the crew could not fetch a doctor and instead prayed for her. According to Johann, they were so angry with Freund that they 'wanted to kill him'.

Johann's final day of shooting included the (eventually deleted) scene in which she played a Christian martyr about to be thrown to lions. While Freund and the crew were safely housed in cages, Johann had to stand before the lions unprotected. Against the pleas of her secretary Ruby Holloway, Johann agreed to the dangerous shot: 'I took a deep breath, praying to the Holy Spirit and to my guardian angel, who were already with me.' She remembered the advice that animals can sense fear in their prey – but by that point, she was too worn-out to feel afraid. 'Those lions saw no fear in me – just tired and exhausted bones… Maybe if I had been a female lion there would have been some response, but the lions were indifferent. No sex appeal there.'

At the end of the ordeal, Johann confronted producer Carl Laemmle Jr. and told him in no uncertain terms that she would never work for his studio again, despite being contracted for another film (an adaptation of Oliver La Farge's novel *Laughing Boy*). Laemmle himself struck her as 'an awfully nice person, a very sensitive man'; indeed, Johann got on well with most of the people involved with the film. She had particular praise for Karloff, who she hailed as 'a great gentleman... very good, very kind' although also harbouring 'a hidden sorrow that I sensed and respected'. For her, Karl Freund was the lone worm in the apple.

Shortly after turning her back on Universal, Zita Johann turned her back on all of Hollywood, which she would later dismiss as an 'ego factory' ('they were selling sex and egos... they patterned their actors to play the same parts all the time'). She appeared in a few more films, culminating in Fox's *Grand Canary* (1934), before resuming her stage career in New York. She made occasional returns to the screen as well, acting as a storyteller in a 1970s pilot for a proposed children's series called *Zita and Friends* and – as a result of being a family friend to exploitation director Samuel M. Sherman – appearing in the 1986 horror film *Raiders of the Living Dead*. By and large, however, Johann spent her later years working as a teacher and writing books, exploring spirituality in novels that sadly remain unpublished.[36]

EDWARD VAN SLOAN, THE HOST

The Mummy shares two members of its principal cast with Universal's *Dracula*: David Manners and Edward Van Sloan, who played Jonathan Harker and Van Helsing respectively in *Dracula* before being cast as Frank Whemple and Dr. Muller in *The Mummy*. Each of them is essentially reprising his role from the earlier film, with Manners playing the nominal hero and Van Sloan as the genial occult expert who helps him. In either case, the Manners character is actually one of the less interesting members of the ensemble and is regularly outshone by the surrounding cast, with Van Sloan offering a more memorable performance than his co-star.

The Mummy's script identifies Muller as 'an elderly man, whose main job is to state the occult premises of the story convincingly and make the audience believe them', adding

Fig 4: Imhotep in coffin

that 'Van Sloan is the ideal man for the part'. Indeed he was, and audiences familiar with Universal's product would have recognised him as such.

As well as *Dracula* Van Sloan had turned up in *Frankenstein*, where he played Frankenstein's teacher Dr. Waldman. This character has a limited role in the story, getting killed during the Monster's escape from the castle, but in terms of personality Waldman is essentially the same as Van Helsing and Muller: a genteel, knowledgeable fellow who understands how dangerous it is to meddle with forbidden forces.

The original release of *Dracula* gave Van Sloan an additional scene at the very end, which was removed from later re-issues but nonetheless entered genre legend. Lifted from the Dean/Balderston stage play, the wry sequence has Van Sloan directly address the audience, expressing hope that they will not have nightmares – only to then assure them that 'there are such things' as vampires.[37] Van Sloan was granted a similar sequence in *Frankenstein*, this time at the beginning of the film, offering a somewhat camp warning of the horrors to follow.[38]

These sequences drew upon the conventions of stage theatre while also prefiguring the concept of the horror host. As a character type, horror hosts came into their own during the 1950s when sundry presenters (ranging from the genial to the ghoulish) were created for radio, television and comics to introduce stories of the macabre.[39]

While Edward Van Sloan appeared in various subsequent films, typically as genteel authority figures, he had only two more horror roles: he returned to the Van Helsing character in 1936 with *Dracula's Daughter* and, atypically, played a villain in the mad scientist serial *The Phantom Creeps* (1939). *The Mummy* shows Edward Van Sloan at the top of his game as Universal's resident horror host – the character who guides audiences through the realm of celluloid occult.

JACK PIERCE, THE MONSTER-MAKER

The commentators who hailed Boris Karloff as the new Lon Chaney had only half of the picture. Chaney devised his make-up himself, but Karloff's most iconic transformations were brought about by Universal's resident cosmetic genius, Jack Pierce.

After initially finding work as an actor and stuntman, Pierce became a professional film make-up artist in 1915. He put his talents on display when he turned actor Jacques Lernier into a simian for the 1926 film *The Monkey Talks*, his work on which caught the eye of Universal. Pierce quickly became a key figure in the studio's horror production, and developed the looks for every major Universal monster through the 1930s and 1940s. It was Pierce who gave Conrad Veidt his terrifying grin in *The Man who Laughs*, Pierce who gave Bela Lugosi a vampiric makeover in *Dracula*, and Pierce who helped to cement Karloff's horror stardom in *Frankenstein*, *The Old Dark House* and *The Mummy*. (Subsequent icons, including the Wolf Man, the Invisible Man and the Bride of Frankenstein, were also Pierce's doing.)[40]

The portrayal of Imhotep, then, was merely one of many triumphs to come from the imagination and ingenuity of Jack Pierce. The make-up included multiple layers of bandages; the lower layer was sealed with tape, while the upper layer – burnt and blackened – was designed to break in a convincing manner as the mummy came to life. As Ardath Bey, Karloff wore a simpler but still striking make-up job. Pierce gave a parchment-like texture to the actor's skin using a mixture of cotton, collodion and fuller's earth. Like the *Frankenstein* make-up, the Ardath Bey make-up was designed to accentuate Karloff's natural visage, particularly his heavy brows.[41]

In a 1935 interview Karloff went into detail about the ordeal he went through as Pierce transformed him into the mummy:

[M]y worst makeup was in *The Mummy*. That took nine hours to get on. There were two makeups in that – one the mummy in the tomb, and the second, the mummy come to life. The nine-hour makeup was the first one. Clay was applied, allowed to dry, then covered in wrappings; then more clay and more wrappings. The second mummy makeup took four hours; it was uncomfortable in the extreme as the wrappings were put on wet and as they dried they tightened, and it was very difficult to speak my lines with my throat so constricted.[42]

For his work on *The Mummy*, Pierce received a Hollywood Filmograph award – which was presented to him by Karloff.[43]

FOOTNOTES

27. Kinsey, W., *Fantastic Films of the Decades, Volume 1: The Silent Era* (Peveril Publishing, Barnby, 2015) p50
28. Skal, D. J., *Hollywood Gothic: The Tangled Web of Dracula from Novel to Stage to Screen* (W.W. Norton, New York, 2004) p184
29. Rubicam, E. R., 'John Balderston: From Ancient Egyptian Tombs to Hollywood Screening Rooms', *Filmfax*, no. 87-88, 2002, pp86-9
30. The development of Universal's *Dracula* script is discussed in Skal, D. J., *Hollywood Gothic: The Tangled Web of Dracula from Novel to Stage to Screen* (W.W. Norton, New York, 2004) and Riley, P. J., *Dracula Starring Lon Chaney: An Alternate History for Classic Film Monsters* (BearManor Media, Albany, 2010).
31. Rubicam, E. R., 'John Balderston: From Ancient Egyptian Tombs to Hollywood Screening Rooms', *Filmfax*, no. 87-88, 2002, pp86-9
32. Kinsey, W., *Fantastic Films of the Decades, Volume 2: The 30s* (Peveril Publishing, Barnby, 2015) pp29, 33
33. Barnum, M., 'The Mummy's Mate: An Interview with Zita Johann', *Filmfax*, no. 65, 1998, pp81-3
34. See Atkins, R., *Guest Parking: Zita Johann* (BearManor Media, Albany, 2015). The part of Dracula's daughter instead went to Gloria Holden.
35. The following description of Johann's ordeal, including relevant quotations, is derived from two sources: Johann, Z. in *The Mummy* (MagicImage Filmbooks, Absecon, 1989) pp19-20; and Barnum, M., 'The Mummy's Mate: An Interview with Zita Johann', *Filmfax*, no. 65, 1998, pp81-3.
36. Johann's post-Hollywood life is covered in more depth in Barnum, M., 'The Mummy's Mate: An Interview with Zita Johann', *Filmfax*, no. 65, 1998, pp81-3; and Atkins, R., *Guest Parking: Zita Johann* (BearManor Media, Albany, 2015). The latter book contains the script for a play she

wrote, *And Then It Was Morning*.

37. Spadoni, R., *Uncanny Bodies: The Coming of Sound Film and the Origins of the Horror Genre* (University of California Press, Berkeley, 2007) p66
38. Matthews, M. E., *Fear Itself: Horror on Screen and in Reality During the Depression and World War II* (McFarland & Company, Jefferson, 2009) p35
39. For discussions of the horror host concept see Daniels, L., *Fear: A History of Horror in the Mass Media* (Granada Publishing, St Albans, 1975) and Skal, D. J., *The Monster Show: A Cultural History of Horror* (Penguin Books, London, 1994). As an aside, Boris Karloff would later take on the role of horror host in the television series *Boris Karloff's Thriller* (1960-1962) and Mario Bava's anthology film *Black Sabbath* (*I tre volti*, 1963).
40. Kinsey, W., *Fantastic Films of the Decades, Volume 1: The Silent Era* (Peveril Publishing, Barnby, 2015) p159
41. Essman, S., *Jack Pierce: The Man Behind the Monsters* (Visionary Media, Glendora, 2000) p14-5
42. Peirse, A., *After Dracula: The 1930s Horror Film* (I. B. Tauris, London, 2013) p33
43. Essman, S., *Jack Pierce: The Man Behind the Monsters* (Visionary Media, Glendora, 2000) p14-5

Part 2: Analysis
Chapter 4. The Egypt of *The Mummy*

The Mummy is a film in which people of the twentieth century interact with ancient Egyptians, either figuratively (through the work of archaeologists) or literally (through the resurrected Imhotep and his machinations). But while it deals with history, *The Mummy* should not be mistaken for a historically accurate film. This fact is neatly encapsulated by the shot of Anck-es-en-Amon's resting place in the museum, where a card gives her period of death as the Eighteenth Dynasty, circa 1730 BC when, in reality, 1730 BC fell within the Fourteenth Dynasty. This error, which possibly arose from confusion between the Eighteenth Dynasty and the eighteenth century BC, turns up consistently throughout the film's dialogue, and indicates that few if any people involved with the production of *The Mummy* cared about the accurate representation of history.

Instead, the ancient Egypt of *The Mummy* is a never-never land, one that had already been visited multiple times by filmmakers. When Ardath Bey calls up images of his past life as Imhotep he is effectively screening a silent movie, and the result would have been familiar to filmgoers of 1932: the Egypt portrayed is one of extravagant processions, imposing structures and an Expressionistic sheen, as in *The Loves of Pharaoh* (1921) and *The Ten Commandments* (1923). When Helen appears in a midriff-baring mock-Egyptian costume she shows only passing similarity to the women depicted in ancient Egyptian art, but fits right in alongside Theda Bara in *Cleopatra* (1917), Carmel Myers in *The Dancer of the Nile* (1923) and Julia Faye in *The Ten Commandments*. The age of 'Tutmania' had inspired fashion designers to utilise scrolls, scarabs, gold and lapis lazuli in capturing the spirit of the Nile;[44] Helen was just one of many modern women to allow an Egyptian touch into their wardrobe.

While verisimilitude was not high on their agenda, the makers of *The Mummy* did borrow freely from actual Egyptology to suit the story and atmosphere of their film. This chapter will examine how *The Mummy* approaches ancient Egypt and the ways in which it reflects contemporary attitudes towards the place and era.

History and Modernity

Although set almost entirely in the Cairo of 1932, *The Mummy* shows little concern with twentieth-century Egypt; indeed, many of the principal characters are not even Egyptian. The central cast is taken up in large part by European archaeologists staying in Egypt for research purposes. Most of the Egyptian characters are granted minor, largely dialogue-free roles as police officers, hotel workers, excavation workmen and museum guards. These last two groups – people charged respectively with digging up and preserving the relics of ancient Egypt – are the most prominent in the film.

The two significant Egyptian characters are Imhotep/Ardath Bey and the half-English Helen Grosvenor, who are likewise defined by their relation to ancient Egypt. Imhotep is, of course, a millennia-old mummy resurrected. Helen is a reincarnation of an ancient princess, and shows contempt for the state of Egypt in the twentieth century. In her very first scene, Helen is introduced gazing out at the pyramids from the Cairo hotel, ignoring the dance going on in the room around her. 'Is there a view like this in all the world, Helen?' asks Muller, strolling over to see her. 'The real Egypt,' she replies in a dreamy manner. She then looks down across the more recent buildings of the city, frowning: 'Are we really in this dreadful modern Cairo?' This line, as written in the shooting script, is distinctly racist: 'are we really in this dreadful Arab city – this modern Cairo?' Later, when she visits Ardath Bey's lair and sees the trappings that adorn it, she delightedly exclaims 'ancient Egypt, nothing modern!'

In *The Mummy*, then, the Egypt of the 1930s is treated merely as a midway point between Western civilisation and the era of the Pharaohs: a land of museums, excavations, archaeologists, and the occasional revived mummy.[45]

The Egypt of *The Mummy* is first depicted through the eyes of three European archaeologists in the prologue: Muller, Ralph Norton and Sir Joseph Whemple. Each of these characters is given a distinct viewpoint which conflicts with those of his comrades. Norton, the youngest of the three, is presented as the voice of boyish enthusiasm, eager to get on with the job; he is contrasted with Joseph Whemple, an older and more level-headed archaeologist. The first line of dialogue in the film is spoken by Norton: 'Trying to teach me a lesson in patience, Sir Joseph?' he asks as they arrange their finds, before griping that the expedition will not win medals from the British Museum. 'We didn't come to dig in Egypt for medals,' replies Whemple. 'Much more is learned from studying bits of broken pottery than from all the sensational finds.' While sound as far as real-life archaeology is concerned, this latter philosophy is not particularly useful for starting a horror film, so it is clear which of the two characters will get his way.

Muller, the other man in the prologue, represents a third point of view. He is an occult expert who believes in the reality of ancient Egyptian magic, and holds that there are some secrets that should remain buried by history. His perspective puts him in conflict with both Norton and Whemple: as the other two prepare to open the box containing the Scroll of Thoth, it is Muller who stops them, drawing attention to the curse engraved on the box.

'Oh, come, Dr. Muller,' implores the eager young Norton, 'surely a few thousand years in the Earth would take the mumbo jumbo off any old curse?' Muller dismisses his youthful comrade ('Ugh, I cannot speak before a boy!') and bids Whemple outside into the desert, to continue the conversation 'under the stars of Egypt'.

'The gods of Egypt still live in these hills, in their ruined temples,' says Muller. 'The ancient spells are weaker, but some of them are still potent. And I believe you have in your hut the Scroll of Thoth itself, which contains the great spell by which Isis raised Osiris from the dead.'

This scene lasts a little longer in the shooting script, which has Muller make a direct appeal to the ancient Egyptian pantheon ('May the gods grant, for your sake, that you have not found the Scroll of Thoth') before preparing to set off into the desert alone, rather than take part in what he considers sacrilege. Of course, as the plot demands, Norton lets his impatience get the better of him and inadvertently revives Imhotep while the other two men are outside. If only he had listened to Muller!

HISTORICAL CONNECTIONS

The spectre of Tutankhamun permeates *The Mummy*. The film's prologue takes place in 1921, the year before the real-life opening of Tutankhamun's tomb, a date likely intended to conjure memories of the discovery. When Ardath Bey leads the 1932 expedition to the tomb of Anck-es-en-Amon, he announces that it will be 'the most sensational find

Fig 5: Noble Johnson as the Nubian

since that of Tutankhamun' – clearly, this mummy has familiarised himself with recent developments in Egyptology since his resurrection a decade beforehand. Reaching the tomb, the archaeologists remark upon the intact seal, again evoking the Tutankhamun discovery. The choice of prop is not accurate, however: while the unbroken seal of Tutankhamun's tomb was a piece of sturdy rope, bound with a small lump of clay bearing the images of kneeling figures,[46] *The Mummy* uses a tablet-like seal adorned with images of jackals. 'The seal of the Seven Jackals,' proclaims Frank Whemple.

A number of historical names turn up during the film, aside from the aforementioned reference to Tutankhamun. There was a historical Imhotep, but he has almost nothing in common with the character played by Karloff. As a man of the twenty-seventh century BC he lived in a different millennium to his film counterpart. Far from dying in disgrace and being erased from history, he was ultimately deified.[47] It could be argued that the character is meant to be a different person who happens to have the same name, but the film's dialogue generally implies that there is only one Imhotep of significance.

The name of the ruling Pharaoh at the time of Imhotep's death is given in the film as Amenophis. This is the Greek form of Amenhotep, a name shared by four Pharaohs, all from the Eighteenth Dynasty; the most significant of them was Amenhotep IV, better known as Akhenaten.[48] The film does not specify which Amenophis/Amenhotep appears in its story.

The name of Anck-es-en-Amon also comes from history, and the real Anck-es-en-Amon (or Ankhesenamun) was indeed the daughter of a Pharaoh Amenophis – specifically, Akhenaten. But she lived in the fourteenth century BC, not 1730 BC; and while the film shows her being outlived by her father, in reality she survived both Akhenaten and her husband, Tutankhamun.[49]

Tutankhamun, as it happens, is the linking factor behind many of the jumbled names and dates used in *The Mummy*. The boy-king lived during the Eighteenth Dynasty, and was the son of Amenophis/Akhenaten and husband of Anck-es-en-Amon.[50] The film appears to have lifted these basic details of Tutankhamun's life and worked them into an almost entirely fictitious story. Naming the central character 'Tutankhamun' would perhaps have been too obvious, hence the interpolation of Imhotep.

When the resurrected Imhotep assumes the name Ardath Bey, a near-anagram of 'Arab Death', this may have been a Hollywood in-joke. The actress Theodosia Goodman was known under the similarly-anagrammatic name of Theda Bara; although she was born in Ohio to a Polish Jewish father and Swiss mother, Bara's career in silent film was accompanied by a press campaign passing her off as the daughter of an Egyptian born in the shadow of the Sphinx.[51]

In designing Imhotep's appearance, make-up artist Jack Pierce used real-life mummies as references, although it is unclear which ones he chose. Some sources indicate that the mummy of Seti II was the model for Imhotep.[52] In her book *The Mummy's Curse: Mummymania in the English-Speaking World*, Jasmine Day cites Seti I and Rameses III as the most likely candidates; she points out how Pierce's design appears to be emulating specific aspects of these mummies that were, in fact, the result of damage by ancient grave-robbers:

> The unexplained absence of Im-Ho-Tep's outer wrappings obscures the causes of similar conditions of actual mummies (including scientific study and interference by tomb robbers), implying that they were interred in this state. Im-Ho-Tep's appearance was copied from the mummy of at least one king: Seti I, if not also Rameses III. Both of these mummies were ravaged by tomb robbers and partly unwrapped in the nineteenth century, both retained only their innermost bandages, their arms wrapped separately and their unwrapped and detached heads reattached by ancient priests

who restored their burials. A cloth that the priests wound around the neck of Rameses III to disguise the damage reappears on Karloff's outfit and Seti I wears a similar 'scarf'. Karloff's costume is probably based at least partly upon Cairo Museum photographs of Seti I. Im-Ho-Tep's hands are unwrapped like those of Seti I, and his head uncovered like those of Seti I and Rameses III, surely practical advantages to Karloff in his costume.[53]

Another possible influence, if not on the physical design of the character, is a mummy that was discovered in 1886 and possibly belongs to Pentaweret, a son of Rameses III who was sentenced to death for plotting to overthrow his father. His mouth agape in what resembles a scream, some have theorised that the individual was buried alive. Margaret Bunson's *Encyclopaedia of Ancient Egypt* describes the facial features of this mummy as being 'distorted in agony, as from convulsion or pain'[54] – a phrase that echoes dialogue from *The Mummy*'s prologue, where the archaeologists discuss the nature of Imhotep's death:

'Looks as though he died in some sensationally unpleasant manner.'

'Contorted muscles show that he struggled in the bandages.'

'Buried alive!'

The Mummy depicts a total of three historical characters abroad in modern Cairo; each is a familiar figure from Hollywood Egypt, and each is transported to the present day through a different means. The most obvious are the magician, Imhotep/Ardath Bey, who arrives via resurrection, and the princess Helen/Anck-es-en-Amon, who arrives via reincarnation. The third is the Nubian, who arrives via regression.

Literature set in ancient Egypt, such as Joseph Holt Ingraham's *Pillar of Fire* (1859), Frederick Myron Colby's *The Daughter of Pharaoh* (1886) and H. Rider Haggard's *Cleopatra* (1889), had long used Nubian slaves as exotic scenery-dressing. When the Paris Opera performed Charles Gounod's *Faust* in the nineteenth century, Cleopatra's shade was accompanied by her slaves: ballet-dancing Nubians.[55]

The Mummy itself shows a group of black men, identified as Nubians in the shooting script, during the flashback sequence. Small wonder, then, that after his resurrection Ardath Bey sets about obtaining a Nubian slave for himself by placing Joseph Whemple's black manservant under his control. This character is played by African-American actor Noble Johnson, who had previously performed such multi-ethnic roles as the Bronze Man in *The Ten Commandments* (1923), the Prince of the Indies in *The Thief of Baghdad* (1924) and Queequeg in *Moby Dick* (1931). The film indicates that the servant's Nubian ancestry makes him susceptible to Ardath Bey's control: 'The ancient blood… so you have made him your slave,' says Muller.

Referred to simply as 'the Nubian' by the other characters and given just one line of dialogue ('yes, effendi') the character is something of a racial stereotype. The film does, at least, deign to preserve his life: while the shooting script has a disgruntled Ardath Bey using his magic ring to strike the unsatisfactory servant dead, the film simply has the Nubian shuffling offscreen to escape his vengeful master, never to be seen again.

RELIGION AND THE SUPERNATURAL

Fig 6: *The Scroll of Thoth*

With its themes of death, resurrection and the afterlife, *The Mummy* frequently touches upon ancient Egyptian religion. Its general practice is to pick bits and pieces of the Egyptians' belief system to suit the needs of its story, all the while taking large amounts of artistic license.

The film establishes its version of Egyptian religion early with a discussion about the 'priests of the temple of the Sun in Karnak' and their practices. Muller states with authority that 'the priestesses of the temple of Karnak were the daughters of the reigning pharaohs... the sacred virgins of Isis'; this concept has a grain of truth, as daughters of pharaohs did serve ritual roles. Many women of high social class in ancient Egypt acted as priestesses, and while the priesthood had become all-male by the Eighteenth Dynasty, women from elite families were still granted positions as temple musicians.[56] The film therefore has justification for giving a religious role to the princess Anck-es-en-Amon. However, the notion that a pharaoh's daughter would necessarily serve as a holy virgin – a role which, in the shooting script, leads to Anck-es-en-Amon's execution for her relationship with Imhotep – is no more than a fantasy invented to fit the film's plot. The usage of the phrase 'vestal virgin' further muddies matters as, strictly speaking, this refers to priestesses of the Roman goddess Vesta.[57]

As well as being buried alive, Imhotep has been barred from the afterlife: Muller, examining the mummy case, remarks that 'the sacred spells which protect the soul in its journey to the underworld have been chipped off the coffin'. This element of the film's cosmology is reasonably accurate, as the ancient Egyptians did indeed inscribe spells onto sarcophagi in an effort to ensure the soul's survival of various hazards on its way to the realm of Osiris.[58]

There is no hard evidence that ancient Egyptian religion involved earthly reincarnation such as the one undertaken by Anck-es-en-Amon, although screenwriter John L. Balderston did make an attempt to tie this notion to the Egyptian concept of the Ka. In the religion of ancient Egypt, the Ka was an individual's life-force or vital essence, sometimes depicted in art as a doppelganger-like double.[59] A line deleted from the film but found in the shooting script has Imhotep remark of Anck-es-en-Amon that 'her Ka may live today, in a body as beautiful as hers was in old Egypt'.

As discussed in Chapter 1, reincarnation had been used as a theme in earlier mummy stories, most notably Bram Stoker's *The Jewel of Seven Stars*. The silent films *When Soul Meets Soul* (1913) and *The Undying Flame* (1917) likewise featured ancient Egyptians being reincarnated. Indeed, by associating reincarnation with ancient Egypt, *The Mummy* was tapping into something of a cultural zeitgeist.

As part of the studio publicity for her film *Cleopatra*, Theda Bara's personal press agent claimed that the heavily-exoticised actress was a reincarnation of the titular queen ('Only one authentic representation of Cleopatra is now extant… and it shows a remarkable likeness to the star of the modern screen').[60] At the time of the film's release, Englishwoman Dorothy Eady had already become convinced that she was a reincarnation of an ancient Egyptian. Her personal journey began with a near-death experience in 1907 when she was three years old, and her childhood passion for the age of the pharaohs impressed the Egyptologist Sir Ernest A. Wallis Budge; she would later move to Egypt in 1933 and change her name to Om Seti.[61]

Christine Campbell Thomson, who edited the popular Not at Night horror anthologies from 1925 to 1937,[62] also believed herself to have spent previous lives in ancient Egypt. Becoming an occult author in later life, she devoted an entire chapter of her 1975 book *A Case for Reincarnation* to her Egyptian memories, including her recollection of awaking in a sarcophagus after being placed into a death-like state by a ritual drug – a scene that could have come right out of a mummy film. She believed that one of her past lives was that of princess Merit-Aton, elder sister of the real-life Anck-es-en-Amon.[63] The ancient Egyptians may not have believed in reincarnation, but people who believe in reincarnation are often keen on ancient Egyptians.

Like reincarnation, the idea of the walking mummy is of dubious relation to the beliefs of ancient Egypt. Some commentators, such as Stuart Tyson Smith,[64] have suggested that the story of *The Mummy* was partly derived from the Egyptian legend of Setma Khāmuas and Nefer-Ka-Ptah.[65]

Recorded on a papyrus circa 233 BC, this story had been translated or retold by multiple authors, including Peter Le Page Renouf (*Records of the Past*, 1875), Lafcadio Hearn (*Stray Leaves from Strange Literature*, 1884) and Francis Llewellyn Griffith (*Stories of the High Priests of Memphis*, 1900) along with multiple French and German writers. The most chronologically-relevant version in regards to *The Mummy* is that included by Sir Ernest A. Wallis Budge in his 1931 volume *Egyptian Tales & Romances*.[66]

Setma Khāmuas, a folk-hero derived from a historical son of Rameses II, figures in a number of legends; this one details Khāmuas' quest for a magic book written by Thoth, god of wisdom. Amongst other things the book allows the user to return from the dead: one of its spells 'will, even if thou art resident in the Other World, enable thee to resume the form which thou hadst upon the earth'.[67] Like its cinematic counterpart, this book of Thoth is carefully hidden, and those who obtain it risk provoking divine wrath. Khāmuas meets the ghost of the book's previous owner, Nefer-Ka-Ptah, and learns that this individual had angered Thoth by stealing the book and was subsequently driven to suicide by divine harassment. Ignoring both this warning and the advice of the pharaoh, Khāmuas steals the book, and proceeds to suffer woes of his own.

But while Budge's introduction says that this tale of Khāmuas involves 'his converse with mummies in a tomb', the three beings the protagonist encounters in Nefer-Ka-Ptah's resting place are spirits, not mummies. This is confirmed towards the end of the story, where it is revealed that the physical remains of Nefer-Ka-Ptah's wife and child are located in different tombs to their ghosts and must be retrieved by Khāmuas. The story does contain a few bodily resurrections, but they are passed over briefly, the most significant coming at the very end: 'Nefer-Ka-Ptah rose and transported himself from his tomb to Coptos, and appeared to Khāmuas in the form of a very aged priest.' This is interesting as an example of Egyptian legend prefiguring the living mummy of modern horror, but Nefer-Ka-Ptah nonetheless bears little resemblance to the figure played by Karloff; it would be a stretch to suggest that the celluloid Imhotep or his successors owe a debt to this ancient ghost.

More credible is the notion that the magic book of the legend – attributed to the god Thoth – inspired the Scroll of Thoth used in the film. But again, this plot device has other, better-known precedents.

One is the text known to Egyptologists as the Book of the Dead, which was introduced in the sixteenth century BC and consists of various spells pertaining to the soul's passage to the afterlife, derived mostly from funerary texts.[68] Copies of the Book of the Dead were placed into coffins, something that has a rough parallel with Imhotep's sarcophagus being buried alongside the box containing the Scroll of Thoth in *The Mummy*. The prop used in the film for the scroll is based directly on the papyrus of Hunefer, a fragment of the Book of the Dead.[69]

It is also worth noting that magical texts associated with Thoth were already part and parcel of Western occult tradition and the weird fiction derived from it. The Greeks identified Thoth with their indigenous deity Hermes, and forged the two into a gestalt figure named Hermes Trismegistus (literally, Thrice-Great Hermes; 'thrice-greatest' or 'three times great' being amongst the appellations that the Egyptians used for Thoth). Numerous occult texts were attributed to this legendary personage, and as late as the seventeenth century Hermes Trismegistus was still regarded as a historical figure, although his status had by then been downgraded from deity to inspired mortal.[70]

The influence of Hermetic occultism survived into modernity, as evidenced by the Hermetic Order of the Golden Dawn. This esoteric society included many prominent occultists of the late Victorian and Edwardian eras, amongst them multiple authors of weird fiction. Algernon Blackwood and Arthur Machen are known to have been members; according to some reports, the secret order also counted H. Rider Haggard, Sax Rohmer and Bram Stoker amongst its number.[71] The old god Thoth was a continued presence and was invoked in the writings of the notorious Aleister Crowley, who led a breakaway sect from the Golden Dawn; Crowley's final major work, published in 1944, was entitled *The Book of Thoth*.[72] Another Book of Thoth turns up in Sax Rohmer's 1918 novel *Brood of the Witch-Queen*, where it is used as a tool by an evil magician before being eventually destroyed.

The Mummy portrays the Scroll of Thoth as an object of considerable vintage, even by the standards of ancient Egyptian artefacts. Ardath Bey identifies the scroll as being pre-dynastic, while the shooting script has Muller claim that the scroll was 'handed down from Pharaoh to Pharaoh and from high priest to high priest from before the First Dynasty of Egypt'. The First Dynasty began around 3100 BC; anything before this is literally prehistoric. Going by the film's chronology, the scroll of Thoth is a Stone Age artefact that predates the pyramids and the Sphinx!

All of this is fanciful, but then, *The Mummy* is a fantasy film, one where the Egyptian gods have objective reality. The scroll in question was, presumably, written by the god Thoth himself and any historical implausibility can therefore be excused – after all, who can argue with the god of knowledge over his homeland's heritage…?

This brings us to the film's handling of the Egyptian pantheon. Six deities are mentioned in *The Mummy*: Amon-Ra, Osiris, Isis, Anubis, Thoth and Bast. The portrayal of these figures is simplified but, for the most part, accurate. Osiris is associated with resurrection,

Isis with protection, Anubis with the guidance of the dead and Thoth with knowledge, while Amon-Ra is identified as the king of the gods, all traits that are reasonably true to the myths.

The one oddity is the film's identification of Bast as the 'goddess of evil sendings', when she was a protective figure in Egyptian religion; Putnam's *Cagliostro* script, in which Bast is a 'kind goddess' associated with fertility, is somewhat closer the mark. Balderston was perhaps confusing the cat-headed Bast with the lioness-headed Sekhmet, a war goddess who was associated with the sending of disease and evil spirits.[73] It is also possible that the film uses Bast in this role simply to give Imhotep a cat motif as an analogue to Dracula's bat motif. Ardath Bey owns a cat which seems to be a familiar of sorts; it appears only briefly in the film but is more prominent in the shooting script, standing by the antagonist as he conducts his black magic – thereby prefiguring the Persian cats that accompany villains in the James Bond films and their various parodies.

The deity playing the largest role in the film's fantasy is Osiris, whose mythical resurrection is mentioned by onscreen text that follows the opening credits. No surviving Egyptian text contains a full account of the Osiris myth; the longest version of the story was instead penned by the Greek writer Plutarch in his *Moralia*.[74] Nina Wilcox Putnam was presumably familiar with this text, as she specifically has the villain showing Helen 'a modern edition of Plutarch's account of Osiris and Isis' in one scene of her February 1932 *Cagliostro, or The King of the Dead* script. In Plutarch's telling, the god Set (or Typhon, as Plutarch refers to him, borrowing the name of a Greek deity) tricks his brother Osiris into entering a chest, whereupon Set seals the lid and sends the chest floating down the Nile. Osiris' wife/sister Isis eventually recovers the box, by which time the occupant is dead. Set then stumbles upon the chest and dismembers Osiris' body into fourteen pieces, scattering them in all directions. Isis travels far and wide in search of Osiris' body parts, and succeeds in retrieving all but one; the penis had already been eaten by fishes, and so Isis makes a replacement. However, this is not the end of Osiris, who returns from the dead long enough to sire a son with Isis prior to taking his place as the ruler of the underworld.

Plutarch's account is somewhat coy as to the nature of Osiris' resurrection, which it describes as a return from the underworld – an ambiguous interpretation. By contrast, the references to the narrative found scattered across Egyptian sources are more vivid, if fragmented. Hymns and pyramid texts describe Isis giving Osiris air with her wings prior to receiving his seed, or breathing new life into his body after restoring its appendages.[75] Artwork at the Dendera temple complex shows Isis in the form of a woman-headed bird flying over the body of Osiris, apparently in the act of giving him life.[76]

The Mummy approaches all of this as a straightforward bodily resurrection performed through the use of magic words, available to anyone with the right scroll. The same spell that allowed the goddess Isis to raise Osiris also allows a young whippersnapper archaeologist to raise the mummified corpse of Imhotep.

THE CURSE OF THE MUMMY

Finally, there is the phenomenon that originally prompted Universal to head to Egypt for inspiration: the cursed tomb. This idea had already embedded itself in popular consciousness by the time The Mummy was made; it even turns up in Boris Karloff's previous horror film, the Mongolian-set *Mask of Fu Manchu*, where archaeologists violate the tomb of Genghis Khan. 'Remember the curse on Tutankhamun's tomb?' asks one of the characters; 'all the people connected with it died soon after its opening.'

The concept of the cursed tomb does have ancient Egyptian pedigree. As well as spells for ensuring safe passage into the afterlife, Egyptian tombs often contained spells to protect the resting place of the deceased from unwanted interlopers, be they grave-robbers or wild animals. These came in a number of forms ranging from symbolic amulets to inscribed curses. Such measures clearly did little to dissuade robbers, however, as plunder was rife throughout ancient Egypt and very few tombs survived into modernity intact. It was common practice amongst ancient robbers to set fire to mummies in what may have been an attempt to lay supernatural forces to rest; on the other hand, this may have been done purely for purposes of illumination.[77]

In his 1976 book *Les Momies* (published in English as *The Cult of the Immortal: Mummies and the Ancient Way of Death*) Ange-Pierre Leca describes an incident from 1905 in which a man named Ali Yunis went missing while exploring the necropolis of Dra' Abu el-Naga'. Others entered the tomb in the hopes of finding him; some died, while the more fortunate were merely overcome with nausea and had to retreat. Later in the century, Egyptian archaeologist Sami Gabra and his assistants were overcome with debilitating headaches while making their initial steps into a Tuna al-Gabal necropolis.[78]

Such occurrences have prompted a number of theories ranging from supernatural malice to a poisonous substance left by Egyptian priests. Leca, meanwhile, pins the blame on the sealed chambers becoming filled with noxious gasses from ancient corpses. No matter how straightforward the true explanation may be, the concept of the cursed Egyptian tomb made its way into the Western imagination, and became firmly lodged there when the discovery of Tutankhamun's tomb brought with it another alleged curse.

The key figure in this modern myth is Lord Carnarvon, who took part in the opening of the tomb in November 1922 and died following a mosquito bite a few months later. According to Carnarvon's son, the man's death coincided with the passing of his pet dog and the lights of Cairo falling dark for three minutes. Over the following years the press eagerly reported on the deaths of individuals associated with either Carnarvon or the newly-discovered tomb. 1929, for example, saw the deaths of Carnarvon's wife Lady Almina and secretary Richard Bethell, along with a boy who had the misfortune to be run over by Bethell's hearse. Estimates vary from retelling to retelling, but in all, more than twenty individuals have been cited in the sensationalist press as possible victims of this curse.[79]

No less a personage than Arthur Conan Doyle lent credence to the curse narrative, commenting that 'an evil elemental may have caused Lord Carnavon's fatal illness'.[80] Another person who played a role in spreading such a notion was Arthur Weigall, a popular Egyptological author who observed the tomb's excavation as special correspondent for the *Daily Mail*. Weigall had a rather ambivalent perspective: he dismissed claims that there was a curse inscribed on the wall of Tutankhamun's tomb, but he acknowledged commenting that Carnavon had about six weeks to live after the latter made a disrespectful joke about performing a concert in the pharaoh's resting place. 'Weigall himself never said that Carnarvon's death was a consequence of a curse,' writes Weigall's granddaughter Julie Hankey, 'but maybe he knew his readers would draw their own conclusions'. Weigall died in 1934, kicking off another round of press speculation.[81]

All of this can be dismissed as coincidence, of course, particularly when the people who managed to escape the alleged curse are considered. As he was the first to violate the tomb one might expect Howard Carter to be amongst the first to go, but he did not die until 1939.[82] Dr. Douglas Derry, the man who unwrapped Tutankhamun's mummy, died peacefully at the age of eighty.[83]

But neither sensation-hungry reporters nor authors of weird fiction could let such trivialities get in the way of a good, eerie story. Nor, indeed, could producers of horror films.

FOOTNOTES

44. Cunningham, P.A. in *Clothing and Fashion: American Fashion from Head to Toe* (ABC-CLIO, Santa Barbara, 2016) p173
45. A rather telling blunder has Frank Whemple say to Helen 'I'd have liked Egypt better if I'd met you there – no such luck'; this despite the fact that he *did* meet her in Egypt, and is currently talking to her in his Cairo home. Apparently, modern Cairo does not count as 'Egypt' in his mind: only archaeological sites earn this distinction.
46. Allen, S. J., *Tutankhamun's Tomb: The Thrill of Discovery* (Metropolitan Museum of Art, New York, 2006) p96
47. Shaw, I. and Nicholson, P., *British Museum Dictionary of Ancient Egypt* (BCA, London, 1995) p139
48. Shaw, I. and Nicholson, P., *British Museum Dictionary of Ancient Egypt* (BCA, London, 1995) pp20-21, 28-9
49. Dodson, A. and Hilton, D., *The Complete Royal Families of Ancient Egypt* (Thames & Hudson, London, 2004) p142-5
50. Ibid.
51. For a full biography, see Genini, R., *Theda Bara: A Biography of the Silent Screen Vamp, with a Filmography* (McFarland & Company, Jefferson, 1996).
52. Coniam, M., *Egyptomania Goes to the Movies: From Archaeology to Popular Craze to Hollywood Fantasy* (McFarland & Company, Jefferson, 2017) p63; Mank, G.W., *Bela Lugosi and Boris Karloff: The Expanded Story of a Haunting Collaboration* (McFarland & Company, Jefferson, 2009) p126
53. Day, J., *The Mummy's Curse: Mummymania in the English-Speaking World* (Routledge, Abingdon, Oxon, 2006) p82. In fairness, the film's shooting script specifies that Imhotep has been partially unwrapped at the time the film begins, presumably by the archaeologists.
54. Bunson, M., *Encyclopedia of Ancient Egypt* (Facts On File, Inc, New York, 2002) p311

55. Osborne, C., *The Opera Lover's Companion* (Yale University Press, New Hale, 2004) p159
56. Robins, G. *Women in Ancient Egypt* (The British Museum Press, London, 1993) pp142-156
57. Takács, S. A., *Vestal Virgins, Sibyls, and Matrons: Women in Roman Religion* (University of Texas Press, Austin, 2008)
58. Brock, E. C. in *Encyclopedia of the Archaeology of Ancient Egypt* (Routledge, London, 1999) pp 321-4
59. Shaw, I. and Nicholson, P., *British Museum Dictionary of Ancient Egypt* (BCA, London, 1995) p146
60. Coniam, M., *Egyptomania Goes to the Movies: From Archaeology to Popular Craze to Hollywood Fantasy* (McFarland & Company, Jefferson, 2017) p32
61. Coniam, M., *Egyptomania Goes to the Movies: From Archaeology to Popular Craze to Hollywood Fantasy* (McFarland & Company, Jefferson, 2017) p127; Wren, C. S., 'Briton With a Sense of Déjà Vu Calls Ruins "Home"', *NYTimes.com*, https://www.nytimes.com/1979/04/17/archives/briton-with-a-sense-of-deja-vu-calls-ruins-home-transferred-to.html
62. Ashley, M., 'Not at Night', *SF-Encyclopedia.uk*, http://sf-encyclopedia.uk/fe.php?nm=not_at_night
63. Hartley, C., *A Case for Reincarnation* (St Edmundsbury Press, Bury St Edmunds, 1985) pp119-126
64. Smith, S. T. *Box Office Archaeology: Refining Hollywood's Portrayals of the Past* (Routledge, London, 2016) pp20-23
65. Spellings of these characters' names vary between translations; 'Setma Khamuas' and 'Nefer-Ka-Ptah' are the versions used by Ernest A. Wallis Budge.
66. Budge, E. A. W., *Egyptian Tales & Romances* (Thornton Butterworth, London, 1935) pp149-169
67. All quotations are taken from Budge's retelling.
68. Budge, E. A. W., *The Egyptian Book of the Dead* (Penguin, London, 2008)
69. Riley, P. J. (ed.) *The Mummy* (MagicImage Filmbooks, Absecon, 1989) p14
70. Baigent, M and Leigh, R., *The Elixir and the Stone: A History of Magic and Alchemy* (Viking, London, 1997) pp20-3
71. Daniels, L., *Fear: A History of Horror in the Mass Media* (Granada, London, 1977) p86-7
72. Bogdan, H and Starr, M. P. in *Aleister Crowley and Western Esotericism* (Oxford University Press, Oxford, 2012)
73. Shaw, I. and Nicholson, P., *British Museum Dictionary of Ancient Egypt* (BCA, London, 1995) pp83, 257; Morenz, S., Egyptian Religion (Methuen and Co, London, 1960) p.268
74. Assmann, J., *Death and Salvation in Ancient Egypt* (Cornell University Press, Ithaca, 2005) p23
75. Assmann, J., *Death and Salvation in Ancient Egypt* (Cornell University Press, Ithaca, 2005) pp24-5, 34-5; Erman, A., *A Handbook of Egyptian Religion* (Archibald Constable and Co, London, 1907) p.34
76. Shaw, I. and Nicholson, P., *British Museum Dictionary of Ancient Egypt* (BCA, London, 1995) p142

77. Spencer, A. J., *Death in Ancient Egypt* (Penguin Books, London, 1982) pp74, 79, 109-111
78. Leca, A-P. *The Cult of the Immortal: Mummies and the Ancient Way of Death* (Granada, St Albans, 1983) pp235-8
79. Leca, A-P. *The Cult of the Immortal: Mummies and the Ancient Way of Death* (Granada, St Albans, 1983) pp238-43
80. Coniam, M., *Egyptomania Goes to the Movies: From Archaeology to Popular Craze to Hollywood Fantasy* (McFarland & Company, Jefferson, 2017) p78
81. Hankey, J. *A Passion for Egypt: Arthur Welgall, Tutankhamun and the Curse of the Pharaohs* (Tauris Parke Paperbacks, London, 2007) pp3-5
82. Dodson, A., in *Encyclopedia of the Archaeology of Ancient Egypt* (Routledge, London, 1999) pp190-1
83. Leca, A-P. *The Cult of the Immortal: Mummies and the Ancient Way of Death* (Granada, St Albans, 1983) p242

Chapter 5. Horror and Fantasy in *The Mummy*

Universal's treatments of the vampire and werewolf themes had specific bodies of folklore to draw upon for inspiration, but as *The Mummy* featured what was for all intents and purposes a new variety of monster, the studio had a blank slate. The film not only introduced audiences to the living mummy Imhotep but also transported them to an entire world of gods, magic and curses. As well as taking inspiration from weird fiction and popular Egyptology, *The Mummy* frequently uses contemporary horror films as reference points, synthesising both old and new to create the latest movie monster. In doing so, it established most of the conventions that would be re-used in later mummy films.

'It Comes to Life!'

Fig 7: Close-up of Karloff as Imhotep

In the original *Cagliostro* synopsis the villain's mummy-like attributes were limited, leaving little indication in the story that the character was meant to look any different from an ordinary human being. This is consistent with the mummy stories of Jane Loudon, Edgar Allan Poe and Bram Stoker where mummies are depicted as being in such perfect states of preservation that – when revived – they resemble flesh-and-blood people rather than gruesome walking corpses.

The mummy motif was taken further in Nina Wilcox Putnam's February 1932 *Cagliostro, or The King of the Dead* script. Here, the main character alternates between looking outwardly human and resembling a shrivelled mummy. The script confirms that he has actually been mummified at some point as his torso is described as bearing 'a terrible scar where the body was once slit open to remove the intestines'. However, Cagliostro is not a resurrected corpse but an immortal man who has never died: by showing him to have been mummified, the story appears to be conflating a means of preserving the body for millennia after death with a means of preserving the body for millennia while alive.

The finished version of *The Mummy* removes a lot of this vagueness about the villain's nature. Gone is the pseudo-scientific explanation of his immortality from the Putnam script; gone, too, is the arcane mummification ritual. In the final film, Imhotep is a mummified corpse brought to life through the magical Scroll of Thoth. This recalls the magically animated mummy in Arthur Conan Doyle's 'Lot No. 249' and became the default concept in subsequent mummy movies.

The physical appearance of Imhotep deserves comment. The stereotyped movie mummy, familiar from sundry parodies, is an actor swathed in bandages with little or no attempt to replicate the appearance of the mummified corpse below. But *The Mummy* does not settle for such a simplistic approach. A viewer who sees the shrivelled, sunken face of Imhotep's corpse as it stands in the sarcophagus could be forgiven for assuming that the mummy is a prop, rather than an actor beneath elaborate make-up. That is, of course, until Imhotep comes to life.

As archaeologist Ralph Norton reads his transcription of the scroll, unwittingly speaking the incantation that restores Imhotep to life, a close-up shows the mummy's eyes opening. The camera pans down as Imhotep lowers his arms in a halting, juddering movement, one after the other, breaking free of his bandages in the process. It then returns to Norton, unaware of the event occurring behind him. The camera pans down to the scroll beside him, and the mummy's hand edges into shot as it picks up the scroll and departs. Norton then turns and sees the mummy, but the audience does not: all we see is Imhotep's hand, the full spectacle being left to our imagination.

As a revived corpse played by Boris Karloff under heavy make-up, Imhotep's clearest cinematic precursor is the monster in *Frankenstein*. Like that character, Imhotep would also fit right in alongside the various automaton-like figures to be found in German Expressionist cinema: the murderous sleepwalker in *The Cabinet of Dr. Caligari* (*Das Cabinet des Dr. Caligari*, 1920), the clay man in *The Golem*, the mechanical woman in *Metropolis*. Each of these films includes a ritualised sequence of the creature coming to life, a tradition carried over to Universal's sagas of animated corpses. When the sleepwalker Cesare awakes in *Dr. Caligari*, the film shows a close-up of his eyes opening as he stands upright in a wooden cabinet: a direct precursor to Imhotep's awakening inside his sarcophagus. Director Karl Freund's involvement with the fantastic cinema of German Expressionism, including *The Golem* and *Metropolis*, is perhaps reflected here.

Upon seeing the resurrected Imhotep, Norton's first reaction is to scream in fright; his second is to laugh. His mind broken, he lets out a hollow, unstoppable guffaw as the mummy — still kept out of shot, and represented onscreen solely by a pair of trailing bandages — heads out of the tomb. Whemple and Muller, hearing the laughter, rush inside. 'He went for a little walk,' exclaims the insane young man. 'You should have seen his face!' The scroll and mummy are gone, the only traces being Norton's partial transcription of the former and a dusty handprint left by the latter. This last detail is a holdover from the *Cagliostro* script, where the dusty residue left by the villain was a clue as to his mummified nature.

That Imhotep drives Norton insane through the sheer horror of his appearance, rather than simply killing the sacrilegious archaeologist, is the sort of inventive touch that later mummy films often lack. The destructive power of fear turns up twice more in the film: when Ardath Bey kills the museum guard off-screen, the police deduce that the man died of shock; later, after Sir Joseph Whemple dies, his sceptical son says to Muller 'don't try and make me believe that this Ardath fellow's a mummy come to life, it was that idea and the horror of it that killed my father'. Dracula has fangs, Frankenstein's Monster has brute strength, but *The Mummy* plays with the idea that its monster is capable of destroying through fear alone.

In essence, it is the prologue more than the remainder of the film that launched the mummy subgenre. The sight of the newly-discovered mummy returning to life and terrorising those who disturbed its slumber is the true core of the cinematic mummy. Cagliostro, the immortal man who turned himself into a living mummy through chemical injections, now seems like a bizarre offshoot rather than the subgenre's starting point.

That said, *The Mummy* does retain one element from *Cagliostro* that may be surprising to modern viewers who are familiar with later mummy films: Imhotep's ability to rejuvenate himself. The prologue ends with him shambling out of his tomb as a shrivelled, bandaged mummy, but when he next appears ten years later, he has transformed into a passable semblance of a living man and is presenting himself as a modern Egyptian named Ardath Bey. 'His face is tanned like leather', says the script; 'it is the face of a mummy, but not unlike that of many Orientals who have lived in the tropical sun all their lives'. Ardath Bey's slow, stiff movements and stated aversion to being touched indicate that he still has something of a mummy's fragility about him. 'If I could get my hands on you, I'd break your dried flesh to pieces,' declares Muller at one point, recognising this trait.

Unlike Putnam's *Cagliostro* script, *The Mummy* never depicts the process of its title character changing from mummy to man. It does, however, show audiences the reverse at the very end: Ardath Bey dissolves from his regular face, to that of the mummy, and finally to a skull before crumbling to pieces on the floor.

The *Cagliostro* script suggests that the villain decays 'by the same method of stop shots which was used in *Dr. Jekyll and Mr. Hyde*'. The final shooting script calls for Imhotep to be destroyed offscreen before Frank and Muller walk in on his smouldering remains, but the finished film returns to the earlier conception of the stop shot decomposition. Putnam's reference point, Paramount's 1931 film *Dr. Jekyll and Mr. Hyde*, actually contains multiple transformation sequences that vary in sophistication (the most-praised effect, in which coloured filters are switched to give the impression of make-up appearing on the actor's face,[84] has no counterpart in *The Mummy*). Putnam was most likely thinking of the scene at the end of *Dr. Jekyll and Mr. Hyde* where the title character lies dying, and gradually fades from Hyde to Jekyll across a series of still shots. The effect as used in *The Mummy* is crude and abrupt; Universal would make a better attempt at the same concept in *The Invisible Man*, where the title character's skull can be glimpsed as he regains visibility on his deathbed.

'But Your Power is Too Strong'

Fig 8: Close-up of Karloff as Ardath Bey

Ardath Bey shows a number of supernatural abilities, although unlike the powers of Dracula, these are not drawn from any particular folkloric source. They are instead chosen to suit the needs of the plot, with some serving as replacements for the technological devices used by Cagliostro in the earlier, more science fictional version of the story. While Cagliostro used a television to spy on his opponents, Ardath Bey conjures images in a pool of water, which he can also use to call up scenes from the past. Where Cagliostro had a death ray, Ardath Bey is able to kill people from afar by uttering incantations while staring at their images in the pool.

The villain also possesses the power of mind control. When he meets the Whemples' Nubian servant, he stares at the man and chants in incantation; this causes the servant to kneel before him, and act as his accomplice throughout the remainder of the film. More significant is Ardath Bey's psychic connection to Helen: when he reads from the Scroll of Thoth and chants the name of Anck-es-en-Amon, he forms some sort of telepathic link with the heroine. She falls into a trance and begins making her way to the museum, likewise chanting ancient Egyptian words and reciting the name of Imhotep; he places her into a similar trance twice more during the course of the film. When Helen returns to the Whemples after being lured to Ardath Bey's lair, Anck-es-en-Amon's personality has begun to resurface in a manner that suggests possession. 'There's death there for me,' says Helen, 'and life for something else inside me that isn't me'.

At four points in the film we are shown a close-up of Ardath Bey staring directly at the camera, his face lit so that his eye areas are bathed in shadow. In two of these instances his eyes are hidden in the darkness, but light up as he exercises his powers; the repeated close-up is otherwise entirely static. The film uses a similar effect, with Karloff's eyes being made to light up, in different close-ups: first when Ardath Bey places the Nubian under his control, the second when he starts to exert his influence upon Helen. A similar but more rudimentary effect was used in *Dracula*, with patches of light being shone onto Lugosi's eyes during dramatic moments.

Fig 9: Ardath Bey and Helen

Ardath Bey's powers of mind-control have multiple cinematic precursors. The most obvious is *Dracula*, where the Count places a number of characters under his control. He compels a concert hall employee to deliver a message, and a nurse to grant him entry to Mina's bedroom; and he lures Mina from her home to his embrace, prior to bringing out a secondary personality in her – a clear parallel to Helen's secondary personality as Anck-es-en-Amon. As well as his erotically-charged attacks on various women, Dracula turns genteel Renfield into a manic, grinning, fly-eating servant (something echoed, perhaps, when *The Mummy*'s Norton goes insane at the sight of Imhotep's resurrection).

Another worthwhile comparison point is the 1931 Warner Bros. film *Svengali*, based on the 1894 novel of the same name by George du Maurier. The film's plot deals with an evil hypnotist – a Polish Jew and therefore an ethnic other, like the Transylvanian Dracula and Egyptian Ardath Bey – who places a young woman named Trilby under his control. In depicting Svengali's hold over Trilby, the film uses similar cinematic language to *The Mummy*. The shot-reverse-shot sequences between the two characters' faces, with an emphasis upon Svengali's eyes, prefigure Ardeth Bey's interactions with Helen. Multiple shots show Svengali's eyes with cataract-like clouding as he exerts his powers, including one that has his eyes illuminated while the rest of his face sinks into shadow. A memorable sequence has Svengali staring out of a window; a tracking shot then passes over a set of Expressionistic rooftops before arriving at the window to the sleeping Trilby's bedroom. Helen's introduction in *The Mummy*, where Ardath Bey in the museum and Helen in the hotel are linked by a primitive whip-pan over the buildings of Cairo, seems a rough-and-ready restaging of this (as described in *The Mummy*'s shooting script the shot is a more elaborate journey across the rooftops of night-time Cairo, which would have been even closer to *Svengali*). The *Svengali* scene leads into Trilby climbing out of bed in a trance and walking to Svengali's home, just as Helen is later lured to the lair of Ardath Bey.

'YOU SEEM TO THINK THAT THING HAS ALL THE DEVILS OF HELL IN IT'

As well as Ardath Bey's inherent powers, the story of *The Mummy* involves a number of objects with magical properties. One is the scarab beetle ring worn by Imhotep: as Ardath Bey, he is sometimes shown raising his ring as he chants incantations that subdue those in his power (Helen, the Nubian) and ward off his enemies. This latter act again recalls *Dracula*, albeit in reverse – Ardath Bey's ring has the same effect on Muller and Whemple that Van Helsing's crucifix has on Dracula.

Where the scarab ring is a symbol of evil power, benevolent forces are represented by the Isis charm. When Frank falls under Ardath Bey's magic, he saves himself by clutching at this protective trinket. The Isis charm is obviously derived from the Osiris charms from Putnam's *Cagliostro* script, although those served the opposite purpose: they were used by Cagliostro to focus his death ray.

Finally, and most significantly, there is the Scroll of Thoth. This artefact is what Alfred Hitchcock would have called a MacGuffin, an object that is important to the characters but of little importance to the audience, who recognise it as no more than a means to drive the plot.[85] That said, the scroll is a remarkably tidy and succinct MacGuffin, encapsulating as it does the key fantasy concepts of the film. Immediately after the opening credits, onscreen text introduces the audience to the magic scroll with a purported quotation:

> This is the SCROLL OF THOTH.
>
> Herein are set down the magic words by which Isis raised Osiris from the dead.
>
> Oh! Amon-Ra—Oh! God of Gods—Death is but the doorway to new life—We live today—we shall live again—In many forms shall we return—Oh, mighty one.

This text establishes the supernatural concepts that drive the film's plot: resurrection, here associated with the myth of Osiris, but later applied to Imhotep; reincarnation, foreshadowing Helen's role in the story; and the scroll itself, which serves as an all-purpose magical agent when the narrative requires.

'IN MANY FORMS SHALL WE RETURN'

The opening card is the first point at which the film waxes poetic about reincarnation. It is not the last, as evidenced by the lines Ardath Bey speaks after showing Helen visions of ancient Egypt:

> Anck-es-en-Amon, my love has lasted longer than the temples of our gods. No man ever suffered as I did for you, but the rest you may not know, not until you are about to pass through the great night of terror and triumph, until you are ready to face moments of horror for an eternity of love, until I send back your spirit that has wandered through so many forms and so many ages.

Yet, despite its poetic treatment it receives, the reincarnation theme appears to have entered the script through the back door, so to speak. The early *Cagliostro* synopsis established that Helen resembled Cagliostro's unfaithful love, hence his obsession with killing her, but did not indicate that she was the dead woman's reincarnation. Later versions of the story replaced the villain's rather weak motivation by introducing reincarnation as a plot element.

Helen's status as the reincarnation of Anck-es-en-Amon may explain her otherwise puzzling role as patient to the occultist Muller. Her introductory scene has Muller describing her as his 'most interesting patient', but the film never clarifies exactly what he is treating her for – nor, indeed, what he would be qualified to treat her for, as there is no other indication that he has a medical background. This mystery may at first seem like a script oversight, but it appears to be deliberate on the part of writer Balderston. His shooting script contains an exchange where Frank Whemple asks about Helen's role as a patient, only for her to conspicuously change the subject:

'Why does Muller call you his "patient"? I never saw a girl who looked fitter than you do.'

'I'm sound as a bell.'

'If you don't want to tell me –'

'Why did I faint in front of that museum? I'd never been there.'

The audience is apparently meant to infer that Helen is of interest to Muller for occult reasons. By this point in the development of horror cinema, heroines were simply expected to have supernatural qualities, to the extent where occult experts could express interest in them before the weirdness had even started.

The film's climax has Helen regain the memories of her past life, losing her present identity and taking on the persona of Anck-es-en-Amon, whereupon she expresses confusion at her new surroundings. 'Your last memory is of me in the hour of your death as I knelt by your bed, 3700 years ago,' explains Imhotep. 'Your soul is in a mortal body, renewed many times since we loved in Thebes of old, but that love is not for us again until the great change.'

The sequence reveals that Imhotep has not only been resurrected, but is now immortal, and can make Helen immortal through the same process that he has undergone – a process of being killed, mummified, and resurrected. This rather convoluted plot element is a holdover from Putnam's script, where it was established at an earlier point that, to sustain his immortality, Cagliostro must be periodically mummified.

Once again, the parallels between *The Mummy* and *Dracula* are hard to miss. Ardath Bey's plan to turn Helen into an immortal mummy like himself resembles Dracula's modus operandi of turning women into vampires. Indeed, the dialogue spoken by Dracula in the earlier film clearly prefigures the text attributed to the Scroll of Thoth in *The Mummy*: 'She will live through the centuries to come, as I have lived.'

The Mummy ties Helen's potential immortality to the myth of Osiris' resurrection, just as it does the broader theme of reincarnation. 'The ancient rite must be performed over thy body,' says Imhotep, 'and then I will read the great spell with which Isis brought Osiris back from the grave, and thou shalt rise again.' According to Imhotep, Osiris himself is involved with this process:

> The gods will receive into the underworld the spirit of Anck-es-en-Amon, but not for long. Osiris will release thy soul. You shall rest for now like the setting sun in the west, but you shall dawn anew in the east as the first rays of Amon-Ra dispel the shadow.

'THE GODS OF EGYPT STILL LIVE IN THESE HILLS'

The Egyptian gods are a recurring presence throughout the film, with multiple deities being invoked during the course of the plot. While the elaborate sequence in the *Cagliostro* script where the gods actually appear onscreen did not make it into the final film, *The Mummy* twice lends physical presences to the old deities through the motif of the moving statue.

The first occurrence is in the flashback to ancient Egypt, where Imhotep steals the Scroll of Thoth from beneath a statue representing the god Amon-Ra. As he does so, the statue suddenly swings its arm – a movement later mirrored by the Pharaoh as he passes judgment – and causes Imhotep to look up in startlement: 'I dared the gods' anger', he narrates.

Fig 10: Statue of Isis comes to life

It is unclear as to whether the statue's movement is meant to be a supernatural phenomenon or some kind of mechanism; after all, the stone cavity below has a mechanised lid that slides open at Imhotep's touch. Less ambiguous is the final scene where, in response to Helen's prayers, a statue of Isis raises its arm — which holds an ankh — and blasts a deadly beam at Imhotep.

Both Karl Freund and Boris Karloff had prior experience with animated statues. *The Golem* revolves around a man of clay, while *Metropolis* has a dream sequence where statues depicting the Grim Reaper and the Seven Deadly Sins come to life. Meanwhile, in its chief moment of supernatural fantasy, *The Mask of Fu Manchu* has a statue of Genghis Khan move its arm to present a sword to Karloff's villain.

Each of these statues is portrayed by an actor in costume; *The Mummy* is more rudimentary, using prop statues with hinged arms. The climactic sequence in the *Cagliostro* script would have been rather more spectacular if filmed as described.

That *The Mummy* treats the Egyptian gods as objective reality demonstrates how the spiritual elements of Universal's horror films are, at the end of the day, interchangeable props. After all, the fact that Van Helsing can ward off Dracula with a crucifix indicates that the Judeo-Christian Deity holds sway over that film's fictional world; yet his counterpart in *The Mummy* hands out a charm of Isis to serve essentially the same purpose, with this goddess stepping in at the last minute to save the protagonists. On the Universal lot, one god is as good as another.

Somewhat curiously, the concept of the curse – one of the main cultural inspirations behind the film – turns out to play a negligible role in the story. Although the box containing the Scroll of Thoth bears the warning that anyone who opens it will suffer death and eternal punishment 'in the name of Amon-Ra, the king of the gods', the script never directly ties this threat to the fates of either Ralph Norton (driven mad by the sight of Imhotep's revived mummy) or Joseph Whemple (killed by Ardath Bey's magic). The mummy is revived by the spell which previously raised Osiris; Ardath Bey invokes Bast to strike down his opponents; and Isis finally intervenes to destroy the mummy – but even as the gods are zapping people left, right and centre, Amon-Ra's curse is all but forgotten. Its one mention after the prologue occurs when Joseph Whemple sees his son courting Helen, after learning that Helen is Ardath Bey's target: 'The curse has struck her, and now through her, it will strike my son.'

'IMHOTEP, IMHOTEP, IMHOTEP…'

As can be seen, *The Mummy* is in large part an assemblage of genre conventions and stock plot elements found across horror cinema and weird fiction of the era. The central character, Imhotep, is likewise a synthetic figure, a convergence of various contemporary threads.

First, he is the living dead. This is a motif that had already been eagerly explored in the relatively new field of horror cinema, producing such iconic characters as the coffin-dwelling Dracula, along with his celluloid vampire kin; Frankenstein's grave-robbed creation; and the undead slaves of *White Zombie* (1932). To this list can be added figures who, while not literally the living dead, certainly have corpse-like aspects: the sleepwalker Cesare in *Dr. Caligari*, the skull-faced Erik in *The Phantom of the Opera*.

Imhotep's undead condition is ultimately a result of his transgressive attempt to resurrect Anck-es-en-Amon, which is defined as an act of blasphemy against the Egyptian gods. The association of villainy with the defiance of God or nature was well-established in the horror genre at this point, as evidenced by the array of mad scientist films released before or shortly after *The Mummy*. The height of Henry Frankenstein's hubris is marked by his declaration that 'in the name of God, now I know what it feels like to be God'. In *The Island of Lost Souls*, Dr. Moreau echoes Frankenstein's sentiments by asking 'do you know what it means to feel like God?' before being slain by his own creations. Dr. Jekyll is told by a mentor that he has committed 'the supreme blasphemy' and subsequently confesses to God: 'I have trespassed on Your domain; I have gone further than man should go.' The Invisible Man, as he lies dying, admits that he 'meddled in things that man must leave alone'.

Despite their similar transgressions, these characters all have different motivations. Frankenstein seeks greater understanding of the universe, and is so consumed by this desire that he has apparently put no thought into exactly what his creation will achieve. Dr. Jekyll's experiments started out as an honest attempt to better himself, and by extension humanity as a whole. The Invisible Man becomes obsessed with the potential for material power offered by his condition. Imhotep, meanwhile, is driven by one thing and one alone: his love for Anck-es-en-Amon.

Love is another recurring theme in the monster pantheon of this era. It manifests in various forms from the childlike curiosity shown by King Kong for Fay Wray's heroine to the sordid desire for control exhibited by the Phantom of the Opera, Svengali and others; even Dracula's appetite for blood is coded in sexual terms, his victims being attractive young women. Sometimes this monstrous lust can be read as symbolic necrophilia: Boris Karloff's Satanist in *The Black Cat* (1934) keeps the preserved body of his dead love in his basement, while Peter Lorre's twisted genius in the Karl Freund-directed *Mad Love* (1935) becomes so obsessed with a beautiful actress that he buys a wax model of her, which he plays with like a doll.

Imhotep's obsession also has its necrophilic element, as he seeks to kill Helen/Anck-es-en-Amon and mummify her body before raising her as an undead immortal like himself. However, the sincerity of his love, and the lengths through which he is willing to go for Anck-es-en-Amon, mark him as more sympathetic than the above examples ('No man has ever suffered for woman as you have suffered for me', acknowledges Helen/Anck-es-en-Amon). He is ultimately a tragic figure.

Most of the classic Universal monsters have a strong element of tragedy: they are often treated as monsters by their peers, and so act as monsters in retaliation. *Frankenstein* is one example of this dynamic, which can also be found in the silent films made by the studio before the horror cycle began in earnest in 1931 with *Dracula*. *The Phantom of the Opera*, *The Hunchback of Notre Dame* and *The Man Who Laughs* each revolve around a character who is disfigured (either through birth defect or wanton mutilation) and so shunned by society.

This touch of pathos was later passed on to Universal's supernatural monsters. Dracula has a melancholy moment where he expresses a desire for death ('To die, to be really dead, that must be glorious… there are far worse things awaiting man than death') while *The Werewolf of London* (1935) and *The Wolf Man* (1941) feature mortals transformed against their will into supernatural killers.

The character of Imhotep is a seamless blend of multiple horror archetypes. He is a walking corpse, a curse victim, a transgressive scientist, a doomed lover, a weary immortal. He is evil enough for audiences to want to see him destroyed, and yet sufficiently sympathetic for them to shed a few tears along the way. He is a concise summary of all that was expected from a good horror villain circa 1932.

FOOTNOTES

84. This process is outlined in Kevin Brownlow's 1998 documentary *Universal Horror*.
85. Adair, G., *Alfred Hitchcock: Filming Our Fears* (Oxford University Press, Oxford, 2002) p51

Part 3: Unwrapping
Chapter 6. Conversations with *The Mummy*: Critical Reactions

When *The Mummy* was screened at the RKO Mayfair cinema on Broadway, the building was adorned with portraits of the glamorous Zita Johann and the mummified Karloff; two of the giant mummy heads had light-up eyes to enhance the eerie atmosphere. The most inspired promotional element involved a life-sized mummy model with a microphone attached: punters were encouraged to 'ask the mummy a question', and those who dared would get a response from a cinema employee on the other side of the microphone, answering all questions in character. Studio publicity organ *Universal Weekly* encouraged cinema proprietors across the country to try similar stunts.

The public was reportedly delighted with the display. 'The crowds jammed around this mummy morning, noon and night, causing such a terrific traffic tangle in front of the theatre that stores alongside complained to the police to move the people' reported *Universal Weekly*.[86] It was the job of professional film critics to see through such sensationalism and offer sober-minded evaluations of *The Mummy*, but they too were intrigued by the central figure of all this showmanship: Boris Karloff, the actor who had been transformed into a living mummy. The *Los Angeles Times* offered a prescient take that foresaw Karloff's future place in the film pantheon:

> Surely the mantle of the late Lon Chaney will eventually fall upon the actor Karloff, whose portrayal of an unholy thing in this film, aided by magnificent makeup, establishes him as not just a good character actor, but a finished character star.[87]

The *Los Angeles Examiner* noted that the lead actor was credited simply as 'Karloff', and made a humorous comparison to Greta Garbo – who, similarly, had managed to shed her first name.[88] The *New York Times* took the crowds around the box office as evidence that 'there is a place for a national bogey man in the scheme of things'.[89]

As for the film itself, however, the critical reception was more lukewarm. The *New York Times* critic Andre Sennwald dismissed much of the film as 'costume melodrama for the children' and pointed out the script's reliance on incantations ('It is comforting to know that Im-Ho-Tep can be stricken dead by murmuring: "Sehotpe-ib-re Mem-mosut

Sit-sekhem," but it is too simple a way out'). Despite this, he found time to praise the scenes showing Imhotep's resurrection and prior burial:

> For purposes of terror there are two scenes in *The Mummy* that are weird enough in all conscience. In the first the mummy comes alive and a young archaeologist, going quite mad, laughs in a way that raises the hair on the scalp. In the second Im-Ho-Tep is embalmed alive, and that moment when the tape is drawn across the man's mouth and nose, leaving only his wild eyes staring out of the coffin, is one of decided horror.[90]

Variety's brief review likewise praised the resurrection scene, stating that 'The transformation of Karloff's Im-Ho-Tep from a clay-like figure in a coffin to a living thing is the highlight', while deriding the rest of the film. The review criticised aspects of *The Mummy* as 'too stagey' and 'over-suggestive of the Hollywood set', while describing Zita Johann's performance as 'always role-conscious'.[91]

The review in Britain's *Hartlepool Northern Daily Mail* ran along similar lines, hailing Imhotep's awakening as a 'spicy bit of horrifics… [which] must be seen to be believed' but complaining that *The Mummy* 'doesn't maintain the diabolic macabre touch with which it starts. Perhaps it errs by over-melodramatization. And once the mummy resumes life on this earth as Ardath Bey, a little of the terror drops from the film--but only a little.' This review is primarily positive, though: 'see the film… a bottle of the horrors is a good tonic.'[92] Rather oddly, the review describes the film as starring 'Karloff as the creature of clay', echoing *Variety*'s description of the mummy as a 'clay-like figure'. Were these two critics simply referring to the fact that Karloff's make-up incorporated clay? Or were they recalling one of the living mummy's folkloric and cinematic precursors – the golem?

Motion Picture Herald spoke of *The Mummy* and its audience in somewhat condescending terms. 'It has that type of romance, which, although far-fetched and entirely visionary, is nevertheless fascinating to feminine patrons,' stated the *Herald*, 'while the mystic unrealism should provide the men folk something new'.[93] John Gammie in *Film Weekly* compared *The Mummy*'s premise to that of an earlier Universal hit: 'Beside the theme of an Egyptian prince coming back to life and taking up his thwarted love affair with the modern reincarnation of his princess where he left off 3,000 years ago, the robot man idea of *Frankenstein* becomes almost conventional!' His overall assessment of the film was negative, however, as he argued that 'strangeness itself is not entertainment' and that 'ability to wear pounds of fantastic makeup is scarcely art'.[94]

The *Washington Post*'s review commented that '*The Mummy* still is not in any sense a horror picture. Only in the startling realism of his makeup does Boris Karloff recall such of his terrifying earlier pictures, say as *Frankenstein*.' Perhaps surprisingly, this statement – which, out of context, could be interpreted as a criticism – was quoted by Universal spokesman S. F. Ditcham in the film's publicity. Indeed, Ditcham made what appears to have been a conscious attempt to portray *The Mummy* as a gentler stripe of horror film in the face of rising unease about the genre's excesses: he also quoted reviews from the *Hollywood Reporter* ('It has most of the thrills of the "shock" picture without the gruesomeness of the cycle') and *Chicago Daily News* ('weird and imaginative and at times beautiful') running along similar lines.[95]

The film may have been tamer than its genre contemporaries, but this would likely have gone unnoticed by younger filmgoers. Annette Kuhn's *An Everyday Magic: Cinema and Cultural Memory* quotes a member of the public who saw *The Mummy* as a child: 'I was sat there, dead quiet. And when they opened the lid and it shows him like, you know, and he moves his hand; well, I let one out! I slid along the seat – I was frightened to death!'[96]

Meanwhile, it is safe to say that critics who had grown tired of horror found little in *The Mummy* to change their opinions. When Herbert Thompson cast a wary eye over horror cinema in the August 1933 edition of *Film Weekly*, he listed Egyptian tombs as just one more backdrop to a genre that had outstayed its welcome:

> A succession of supposedly spine-chilling pictures have run the gamut of old dark houses, resuscitated corpses, Egyptian tombs, and ghosts that walk in the night. Every possible and impossible device for inducing gooseflesh and sending cold shivers down the filmgoer's protesting back has been studiously employed by Hollywood's thrill factory. The horror film, in short, has been pumped dry of horrors.[97]

Re-Evaluation

In his 1977 retrospective of vintage horror, Denis Gifford – a respected horror historian of his day – echoed the derisive reviews that *The Mummy* received upon its initial release:

> *The Mummy*… did disappoint, and still does. Sold as a Horror film, it cheats the thrill-seeker by having but two classic moments of horror, both of them brisk: the revival of the emaciated mummy when the words of the sacred Scroll of Thoth are spoken, and the climactic converse when Karloff crumbles again. Sandwiched between these scenes is a mysterious romance between the wizened revival and his reincarnated love. *Mask of Fu Manchu* was meatier by far, with its succession of terrible tortures.[98]

Gifford's assessment ran contrary to the consensus of the 1970s. By this point, admirers of the horror genre had reappraised *The Mummy* and their commentary tended towards the positive.

In his genre study *Fear: A History of Horror in the Mass Media* (1975), horror author Les Daniels hailed the film as 'subtle' but 'powerful'.[99] Alan Frank's *Monsters & Vampires* (1976) likewise offered brief but favourable comments on *The Mummy*, praising Freund's direction and Karloff's performance.[100] Carlos Clarens' *An Illustrated History of the Horror Film* (1967) commented on the film's 'careful photography' and the presence of Karloff in 'one of his most restrained performances', stating that the film 'is notable for its sobriety and refusal to shock'.[101]

A particularly enthusiastic treatment of *The Mummy* is found in William K. Everson's 1974 book *Classics of the Horror Film*. Dismissing most of the mummy subgenre as no more than repetitive variations on a weak premise, Everson spotlighted the 1932 original as the one masterpiece of the cycle. 'The finest sequence in the film is when the Mummy comes back to life' he said, reaffirming critical consensus. 'It is also perhaps the only scene in the entire 40-year Mummy saga that is genuinely horrifying.' He praised the film as being 'beautifully directed by Karl Freund… indicating more than once how much better a film *Dracula* might have been had Freund directed it instead of just photographing it'.

After listing the shortcomings of later mummy films, Everson stated that 'the original

The Mummy instinctively sensed these problems and aimed not at creating *greater* thrills than *Frankenstein*, but different ones. *The Mummy* offered uneasy thrills, not shocks.' As well as setting it apart from the rest of the mummy subgenre, Everson argued, the film's reticence gives it a specific place in the horror canon:

> *The Mummy* can be interpreted as a love story almost as much as a thriller. The menace lies not so much in what the Mummy does, as in the intangibles of Egyptian religion and science that make such happenings possible. Moreover, Karloff's reincarnated Mummy is a being of dignity of whom one feels some compassion, and his ultimate destruction is tragic as much as it is a triumph for the traditional forces of 'good.' [...] Considering how early it came in the horror film cycle, it is surprising how restrained and unsensational *The Mummy* is. On the other hand it is that very restraint that helps to make it a classic. If one accepts *The Bride of Frankenstein* for its *theatre* and *The Body Snatcher* for its literacy, then one must regard *The Mummy* as the closest that Hollywood ever came to creating a poem out of horror.[102]

The Mummy also received erudite commendation from one of the rising talents in British horror fiction: Ramsey Campbell, who penned the introduction to the film's 1977 novelisation. Being a contributor to an official tie-in Campbell was, of course, obliged to speak positively about the film; but still, his assessment shows a sincere respect for the traditions from which *The Mummy* arose. As well as discussing the film in the context of horror cinema, Campbell compared *The Mummy* to horror literature, particularly the influential pulp magazine *Weird Tales*:

> Depending on one's viewpoint, the story was more—or less—than a horror tale: it was a romance of reincarnation, the kind of mixture of the love story and the occult that was popular in *Weird Tales* and its fellow pulp magazines of the period [...] Like the best of the pulps, *The Mummy* benefits from its belief in its own melodrama. Nowhere is there a suggestion of conscious camp, and the occasional potentially embarrassing line is saved from itself by the playing and the direction. No other film has caught the mood of this kind of *Weird Tales* theme so accurately.[103]

Like Everson, Campbell praised the comparative subtlety of the film, favourably comparing the restraint of the resurrection scene with its counterpart in the 1959 Hammer *Mummy*.

This, then, was *The Mummy*'s claim to fame during the 1970s: that it was the most understated, poetic and atmospheric of the Universal horror films. But this selling point was heading for a decline in value. At the time that Everson and Campbell were writing, horror cinema was experiencing a boom in extreme, boundary-pushing films represented by the likes of *Night of the Living Dead* (1968), *The Last House on the Left* (1971), *The Texas Chain Saw Massacre* (1974) and *Cannibal Holocaust* (1980). As films such as these entered the canon, *all* of the Universal classics began to feel understated and poetic by comparison. *The Mummy* no longer stood out.

LATER EVALUATIONS

James Marriott and Kim Newman's *Horror: The Definitive Guide to the Cinema of Fear* (2006) has a dismissive entry on *The Mummy* in which Marriott praises certain aspects of the film, including (once again) the prologue's resurrection scene, but also complains that it merely 'retreads *Dracula* territory… without once returning to the mummy's iconic image'. He singles out one line of dialogue in particular – 'I'm a priestess of Isis! Save me from the mummy – it's dead!' – to sum up the script's 'absurdities'.[104] David J. Skal's *The Monster Show: A Cultural History of Horror* (1994), which explores how the horror genre reflects contemporary society, finds little to analyse in *The Mummy*: Skal treats the film merely as a *Dracula* rehash, 'a good example of the kind of creative conservatism that the studio system fostered'.[105]

Sentiments such as these may suggest a return of the negative consensus from the film's initial release, but *The Mummy* had become too much of an institution to suffer such a fate. The film's position as the start of a subgenre – not to mention the involvement of celluloid icon Karloff in a relatively early horror role – has ensured that *The Mummy* retains immortality as a popular culture artefact. Critics may continue to find weaknesses, but they also continue to find rewarding new ways of approaching the film.

It is *The Mummy*'s status as artefact that Alison Peirse explores in her book *After Dracula: The 1930s Horror Film* (2013) where she positions the film as a cultural memory, one evoked by later mummy films. More than that, Peirse argues, *The Mummy* is itself a film about memory:

Whether it is horror or love that is explored through the ages, *The Mummy* is imbued with remembrance. It is organised through memory-making flashbacks and photography, it evokes cultural recollections of mummy unrolling and Egyptomania, and plays upon the expectations of an audience assumed to have seen *Dracula*.[106]

Barry Keith Grant in *Planks of Reason: Essays on the Horror Film* (1984) attempts to dig deeper. He relates *The Mummy*'s supernatural themes of death and resurrection to the mythological theories in James George Frazer's *The Golden Bough*, while taking a psychoanalytic approach to the film's gender dynamics. In Grant's reading, *The Mummy*'s climax 'implies that it was not enough for Helen simply to reject Imhotep, that she had to integrate her Helen and her Anckesenamon [sic] aspects in order to come into her full power'. His analysis continues:

> What this shows is that there is no safety in ignoring the Id/Underworld/monster (the attitude of the ineffectual patsy in most horror films, e.g., the mayor in *Jaws* and Helen's modern boyfriend [David Manners] in *The Mummy*) but that there is considerable strength in confronting the danger and surviving that deeply acknowledged contact--in other words, re-owning the projection. In this sense horror films are valuable and cathartic, for they may offer the possibility of participating in the acting-out of an unacknowledged wish or fear in a context of resolution rather than repression. This is of course what happens to Helen and not to the Mummy. He is a walking repetition compulsion, determined to complete his frustrated sacrilege and consummate his romance (the sexist aspects of all this are quite blatant in the film).[107]

The topic of gender was later picked up in Rhona J. Berenstein's *Attack of the Leading Ladies: Gender, Sexuality, and Spectatorship in Classic Horror Cinema* (1996). Berenstein examines *The Mummy* as part of a cycle of films in which women are hypnotised, her main comparison point being *White Zombie*. She observes that 'While the prizes won by heroines under hypnosis involve trade-offs—love at the cost of life, in the case of *White Zombie*—those trade-offs often pale in comparison to the gains.' In Berenstein's analysis, Helen Grosvenor 'not only experiences horrible terrors, especially in the final moments of the film in which she comes close to perishing in a vat of boiling fluid, but hypnosis also ensures that she looks great, feels wonderful, journeys through her past life in Egypt, and bonds with a fiend that was once the man of her dreams'.[108] Like Planks' reading,

Berenstein's analysis touches upon the way in which horror films can offer audiences transgressive thrills by exploring the attractive aspects of rule-breaking before normalcy is restored. In this case, normalcy is represented by the hero Frank Whemple, whom Berenstein dismisses as a pale character in comparison to the fascinating Ardath Bey.

Berenstein's book goes on to discuss how Zita Johann was described in exoticised terms by studio publicity. This brings us to one of the most obvious angles of analysis when it comes to Universal's film of a fantasy Egypt: how *The Mummy* portrays culture and race. After all, the entire mummy subgenre is based upon a clash of cultures, pitting Western archaeologists against the mysteries and secrets of ancient Egypt. As the subgenre developed, it repeatedly turned to a stock narrative of rational and noble Westerners battling irrational and vengeful Egyptians, a storyline wide open to accusations of prejudice.

And yet, the original 1932 *Mummy* has not been a particularly significant target of such censure. Jack G. Shaheen's 2003 book *Reel Bad Arabs: How Hollywood Vilifies a People* discusses the stereotypes found in mummy films and pours particular scorn upon the turn-of-the-millennium revivals *The Mummy* (1999) and *The Mummy Returns* (2001), but its discussion of the 1932 film is comparatively brief, with Shaheen describing the film as a 'classic' and praising it on formalistic grounds.[109] Moving from race to the broader topic of historical culture, Jon Solomon's *The Ancient World in the Cinema* (2001) comments that director Karl Freund and make-up creator Jack Pierce had 'probably never heard of Akhnaton or Horemheb' but nonetheless hails them as 'creative geniuses' and argues that '*The Mummy* effectively projects the cold, mysterious atmosphere surrounding the Egyptian belief in life after death'.[110]

On the whole, *The Mummy* has managed to stand firm despite early critical indifference and subsequent changes in audience tastes. Whatever objections can be directed its way, the film retains an undeniable appeal – as evidenced by how many imitations and attempted revivals it has inspired over the decades. The final chapter of this book will demonstrate the full legacy of *The Mummy* by exploring the subgenre that surrounds this seminal film.

FOOTNOTES

86. Riley, P. J. (ed.) *The Mummy* (MagicImage Filmbooks, Absecon, 1989) pp32-33
87. Mank, G. W., *Women in Horror Films, 1930s* (McFarland & Company, Jefferson, 1999) p186
88. Ibid.
89. Sennwald, A. D., 'Life After 3,700 Years', *NYTimes.com*, https://www.nytimes.com/1933/01/07/archives/life-after-3700-years.html
90. Ibid.
91. Anonymous, 'The Mummy', *Variety.com*, http://variety.com/1932/film/reviews/the-mummy-1200410684/
92. Anonymous, 'Hartlepool Northern Daily Mail - Tuesday 30 May 1933', *BritishNewspaperArchive.co.uk*, https://www.britishnewspaperarchive.co.uk/viewer/bl/0000378/19330530/063/0002
93. Grant, B. K. (ed.) *The Dread of Difference: Gender and the Horror Film* (University of Texas Press, Austin, 2015) pp153, 167
94. Gifford, D., '1933 – Masters of Menace', *The House of Hammer*, vol 1, no 11. 1977, pp20-5
95. Johnson, T., *Censored Screams: The British Ban on Hollywood Horror in the Thirties* (McFarland & Company, Jefferson, 1997) p77
96. Kuhn, A., *An Everyday Magic: Cinema and Cultural Memory* (I. B. Tauris, London, 2002) pp87-92
97. Gifford, D., '1933 – Masters of Menace', *The House of Hammer*, vol 1, no 11. 1977, pp20-5
98. Ibid.
99. Daniels, L., *Fear: A History of Horror in the Mass Media* (Granada Publishing, St Albans, 1975) p144
100. Frank, A., *Monsters & Vampires* (Octopus Books, London, 1976) pp99-100
101. Clarens, C., *An Illustrated History of the Horror Film* (G. P. Putnam's Sons, New York, 1967) p73
102. Everson, W. K., *Classics of the Horror Film: From the Days of the Silent Film to The Exorcist* (The Citadel Press, Secaucus, 1974) pp88-93
103. Campbell, R., in *The Mummy* (Berkley Publishing Corporation, New York, 1977) pp v-ix
104. Marriott, J. in *Horror: The Definitive Guide to the Cinema of Fear* (Andre Deutch, London, 2006) p37
105. Skal, D. J., *The Monster Show: A Cultural History of Horror* (Penguin Books, London, 1994) p168
106. Peirse, A., *After Dracula: The 1930s Horror Film* (I. B. Tauris, London, 2013) pp14-36
107. Grant, B. K., *Planks of Reason* (Scarecrow Press, Metuchen, 1984) pp12-14
108. Berenstein, R. J., *Attack of the Leading Ladies: Gender, Sexuality, and Spectatorship in Classic Horror Cinema* (Columbia University Press, New York, 1996) pp109-13
109. Shaheen, J. G., *Reel Bad Arabs: How Hollywood Vilifies a People* (Arris Books, Moreton-in-Marsh, 2003) pp25, 332-42
110. Solomon, J., *The Ancient World in the Cinema* (Yale University Press, New Haven, 2001) p251

Chapter 7. The Legacy of *The Mummy*

The Mummy is the centre of its subgenre. As discussed in the first chapter, the film has around a century's worth of weird fiction behind it; but moreover, it has nearly a century's worth of mummy media in front of it. Ever since the 1930s the plot elements and iconography of *The Mummy* have been re-used, re-interpreted and re-worked in myriad forms.

Universal's Subsequent Mummy Films

Fig 11: The Mummy's Hand

Universal's follow-ups to *The Mummy* began eight years after the original film came out, by which time the studio's horror output had lost some of its spark from the early half of the 1930s.

First came *The Mummy's Hand* in 1940. This film's main innovation is in splitting Imhotep and Ardath Bey – that is, the animated mummy and the fez-wearing magician – into two separate characters; the latter role is given to George Zucco as Professor Andoheb of the Cairo Museum. The film opens with Andoheb tending to his dying father, who passes down to him the ancient knowledge of Karnak's priests. Namely, he shows Andoheb how to resurrect the mummy of Kharis – played by cowboy actor Tom Tyler, with eyes blacked out through special effects – and send it after any troublesome archaeologists who violate the local tombs. Instead of the magic scroll from the first film, the resurrection process involves feeding the mummy a fluid made from extinct 'tana leaves'. This element was possibly inspired by Arthur Conan Doyle's 'Lot No. 249', where the mummy-keeper Bellingham burns balsamic leaves to create an odour; it also recalls the animation of the golem in Jewish folklore and silent German cinema.

The notion of the mummy as golem-like automaton is hinted at in the original film, when Ardath Bey states that he could theoretically resurrect Anck-es-en-Amon's mummy as a soulless puppet, but *The Mummy's Hand* makes fuller use of the idea. The film also spends more time on the curse theme: while Ardath Bey actively encouraged archaeologists to dig up the tomb of Anck-es-en-Amon, Andoheb and Kharis are focused more on driving away grave-robbers, something that later became a conventional motivation for mummies and their sorcerous masters.

Beyond these changes *The Mummy's Hand* goes over so much of the same ground as *The Mummy* that it could be considered a remake as much as a sequel. The opening has Andoheb's father using a pool to conjure up a flashback sequence, as did Karloff's character in the original film. The flashback tells the backstory of Kharis, which is almost identical to that of Imhotep: Kharis committed sacrilege in trying to resurrect his beloved – Ananka, daughter of Pharaoh Amenophis – and was mummified alive as punishment. Indeed, the sequence actually consists mainly of recycled footage from *The Mummy*, with Karloff replaced by Tyler in close-ups but still visible in long shots.

Where the first film reserved the mummy's discovery and resurrection for its prologue, *The Mummy's Hand* uses it as the main thrust of the story. It follows archaeologist Steve Banning and his comrades as they hunt for the tomb of Princess Ananka, but instead find the mummy of Kharis. Andoheb then begins picking off the interlopers by sending a turbaned henchman to place bottles of tana fluid in their tents; like a desperate drug addict, the murderous mummy goes wherever the fluid is to be found. Unlike Imhotep, who was implied to be a fragile being capable of slaying only through magic, the mummy of Kharis possesses superhuman strength and can easily overpower any foe.[111] The film's climax has Andoheb kidnap heroine Marta and try to inject her with the tana fluid to turn her into his immortal lover; as *The Mummy's Hand* dispenses with its predecessor's reincarnation subplot, Andoheb's only motive for doing so is that he finds her pretty.

The film completely lacks the subtlety and restraint of *The Mummy* and instead falls back on action-oriented set pieces and broad comedy wherever possible. The first act is played almost entirely for laughs, thanks to Banning's bumbling sidekick and Marta's stage magician father. Unlike the mysterious and alluring Helen Grosvenor, Marta herself is a feisty foil straight out of a screwball comedy. The tragic aspect of *The Mummy*'s story, with Imhotep searching for his dead love, is replaced with one-note villainy: if Andoheb had a moustache, he would have spent much of his screentime twirling it. But whatever its flaws *The Mummy's Hand* established an enduring image of the mummy movie – that of the shambling revenant vengefully protecting its grave as it slays sacrilegious archaeologists one by one at the behest of an evil Egyptian magician. *The Mummy* may have initiated the cycle, but *The Mummy's Hand* further defined its conventions.

The film ends with Banning setting Kharis ablaze as the mummy laps up spilled tana fluid. Despite his apparent destruction Kharis returned in a string of sequels, with Lon Chaney Jr. stepping into the bandages and the brash comedy replaced with more conventional melodramatics. *The Mummy's Tomb* (1942) takes place thirty years after its predecessor and has the elderly Andoheb passing custody of Kharis onto a younger Egyptian named Mehemet Bey. This new villain takes the mummy to America and revives it to pick off Stephen Banning and his family; being structured around a cast of characters getting offed one after the other by a hulking, bulletproof killer, the film is a clear precursor to the bodycount slashers that would later dominate horror cinema. Mehemet Bey also seeks to prolong his priestly lineage, and so kidnaps heroine Isobel – fiancée of Stephen Banning's dashing son John – in the *de rigueur* attempt to create an immortal bride, only to be shot dead before completing his scheme. Finally, in a conclusion that owes a good deal to *Frankenstein*, Kharis meets a fiery end after being chased into an empty building by a torch-wielding mob.

Torch-wielding mobs never stopped a commercially-viable monster, however. *The Mummy's Ghost* was released in 1944; as well as continuing the exploits of Kharis, this film borrows the reincarnation subplot from the original *Mummy*. The opening sees Andoheb choosing another protégé, Yousef Bey, and sending him to retrieve the mummies of Kharis and Princess Ananka from America. However, it turns out that

Ananka has since been reincarnated, an occurrence signified (rather awkwardly) by her mummy having vanished from under its wrappings. The new host of the princess's soul is Amina, an Egyptian-American college student who has a tendency to sleepwalk and gains a Bride of Frankenstein-style white streak in her hair every time she sees Kharis. Like his predecessors, Yousef Bey apparently cannot be in the same room as an attractive woman without trying to make her immortal, but his designs on Amina end when he is killed by the jealous Kharis. The film's unusually downbeat conclusion has Amina herself turning into a withered mummy as Kharis carries her into a swamp, the ancient lovers finally reunited as they sink beneath the murk.

This conclusion meant that the series now had two mummies to play with. The next outing, *The Mummy's Curse* (1944), takes place twenty-five years after *The Mummy's Ghost* and relocates that film's swamp from New England to Louisiana with no explanation. Kharis is retrieved by yet another fez-wearing magician, who houses the mummy in a repurposed monastery. Ananka is later disturbed by workmen and revives in a striking sequence where she judders her way out of the dried-up swamp, her hardened face making her look like some crude clay doll. This moment shows the genuinely uncanny touch which is missing from so many of the later-period Universal horrors. After a dip in a sunny pool, her skin regains its youthful vitality and she passes herself off as a modern American girl. The magician naturally tries to make her immortal, but gets distracted and succeeds only in turning her back into a mummy. Finally, Kharis smashes the monastery down on himself and the other villains in a tantrum, just as Frankenstein's Monster ruined many a laboratory.

These films all suffer from thin plots and undistinguished direction, but an equally fatal flaw lies with the central character. Kharis may be gifted with immense strength, but as he shuffles slowly from one victim to another it becomes patently obvious that anyone with functioning legs would have no trouble outrunning him. The films repeatedly resort to showing victims paralysed with fear or stumbling into dead ends, obvious contrivances which make the subgenre seem tired even at this early stage. Mummies had clearly gone downhill since the days of 'Lot No. 249', where the Egyptian revenant was capable of bounding over walls.

Indeed, one scene of The Mummy's Curse appears to be a deliberate self-parody: Kharis sneaks up behind the heroine as she puts on her coat, only for her to escape by casually walking away and getting into a car, completely oblivious to her bandaged pursuer as he is left flailing wildly in frustration. If this was intended as a self-deprecating joke it prefigured the next step which Universal's Mummy series was to take. In the late forties the studio's supernatural horror films were falling out of favour, and eventually ended up as a cycle of out-and-out spoofs starring comedy duo Bud Abbott and Lou Costello beginning with 1948's Abbott and Costello Meet Frankenstein. The last of these horror parodies was Abbott and Costello Meet the Mummy (1955), in which the two comedians tangle with grave-robbing crooks; both Abbott and one of the villains meet the mummy ('Klaris, prince of evil') while disguised as mummies themselves. Although this film is not the worst of the batch, it lacks the gleeful energy of Meet Frankenstein.

THE HAMMER MUMMY

Fig 12: Poster for Hammer's 1959 The Mummy

Three years after Abbott and Costello met the mummy, Britain's Hammer Films – which had already produced handsome full-colour adaptations of Frankenstein and Dracula – obtained full remake rights to the Universal horror filmography. The first fruit of this alliance was Hammer's 1959 film The Mummy, directed by Terence Fisher.[112]

Hammer was the ideal studio to take over the series. Under Universal the *Mummy* films had descended into stories about clean-cut heroes against pantomime villains, with no hint of the conflicted scientists or misunderstood monsters that characterised the studio's earlier horror output. Hammer's horrors likewise tended to fall back on good-versus-evil narratives with no shades of grey, but the stories were told with a level of conviction missing from Universal's weaker efforts.

Despite its title, Hammer's *The Mummy* is in most part a remake of *The Mummy's Tomb*. It re-uses that film's story of the magician Mehemet Bey smuggling Kharis out of Egypt to slay John Banning, son of the archaeologist who desecrated the tomb of Ananka. However, it does borrow from other films in the Universal cycle, including the original. The film's prologue mashes together elements from both *The Mummy* and *The Mummy's Hand* by having Stephen Banning revive Kharis by reading from a magic scroll (no tana leaves here) after which Joseph Whemple discovers him a gibbering lunatic. The swampy climax, meanwhile, arrives via *The Mummy's Ghost*. Favouring period settings for its horror, Hammer transplanted the non-Egyptian scenes from 1940s America to 1890s England.

Reuniting the double-act from its *Dracula* and *Frankenstein* films, Hammer cast Peter Cushing as Banning and Christopher Lee as Kharis; meanwhile, George Pastell donned a fez to portray the evil magician while French actress Yvonne Furneaux was cast as both Ananka and her modern-day counterpart Isobel. As with many of Hammer's horror revivals, the main appeal of the film lies in seeing a classic monster in glorious Technicolor along with the lashings of gore afforded by an X certificate. Offsetting the viscera is a stately historical flashback longer and more lavish than those found in the Universal films, if lacking their Expressionistic flair. Hammer's *Mummy* also comes up with some worthwhile alterations to the formula, such as its decision to give Peter Cushing's protagonist a bad leg – thereby making Christopher Lee's relatively agile mummy a more convincing opponent.

A subtext that had been growing in prominence throughout the Universal films becomes plain in the 1959 *Mummy*: the demonisation of ancient Egyptian religion. The 1932 original portrays the Egyptian pantheon as containing both bad and good, the latter represented by the protective deity Isis. The Kharis cycle, on the other hand, equates the Egyptian gods squarely with evil: they are worshipped by the various villainous priests, and offer no protection to the heroes. This is particularly clear in *The Mummy's Curse*, where the evil priest takes over a Christian monastery as his hideout after killing the pious proprietor. Hammer's *Mummy* takes this a step further by having Banning lecture his fez-wearing adversary on the inferiority of ancient Egyptian religion, represented by the cult of the god Karnak.

'Their standard of intelligence must have been remarkably low', says the hero. '[Karnak] was insignificant. He had nothing to commend him to anyone with the slightest degree of intelligence… I made an extensive study of this so-called religion that's based upon artificial creeds and beliefs, some of them ludicrous in the extreme.' Banning also tells the villain that 'the history of your country is steeped in violence,' apparently forgetting the fact that the same can be said of any country. The civilised British Empire is pitted against the barbarism of Egypt, and when the mummy gets gunned down during the climax, it is clear which side comes out on top. Produced less than three years after the Suez crisis, the film perhaps reflects the cultural anxieties of its period.

Of course, Hammer's Egyptology is even less convincing than that of Universal: Karnak is actually the name of a temple complex, rather than a deity. Screenwriter Jimmy Sangster appears to have misinterpreted the references to 'priests of Karnak' that cropped up in the Universal series.

Hammer returned to the mummy theme three times, although none of these films were direct sequels to the 1959 *Mummy*. *The Curse of the Mummy's Tomb* (1964), in contrast to its reactionary predecessor, shows a markedly subversive attitude towards the mummy formula. The discovery of the mummy leads to a three-way argument: the Egyptian character wants it to stay in its tomb; the English archaeologists want it in a museum; and the expedition's boorish American financier, a disciple of P.T. Barnum, wants to make a mint showcasing the mummy as a carnival attraction. The film makes some digs at the sensationalism of Egyptomania, as when the financier gets onstage and talks of curses – prompting a round of smirks and eye-rolls from his audience. He later ends up as the mummy's first victim.

Possibly inspired by the mythical battle between divine siblings Osiris and Set, the film replaces the traditional backstory of forbidden love with a conflict between two princes named Ra and Be (who are identified as the sons of Ramses VIII, a rare case of a specific historical personage being worked into the plot of a mummy film). It is Prince Ra who returns as a mummy, once again controlled by a magician, but the film has a trick in store: the character of the stern-faced Egyptian (again played by George Pastell) turns out to be a red herring. The true villain is the Englishman Adam Beauchamp, who – in another twist – is actually Prince Ra's evil brother, sentenced to eternal life for his fratricide. While this character has none of Karloff's gravitas as Ardath Bey he is a far more inspired creation than the underwritten villains of the Kharis cycle. Ra, meanwhile, is an effectively creepy screen presence, largely due to his habit of emitting deep, muffled breaths of the type later associated with Darth Vader.

Hammer's third mummy film, *The Mummy's Shroud* (1967), marks a step backward. Well-mounted but dull, the film deals with archaeologists discovering the tomb of Prince Kah-to-Bey (whose backstory, involving a murdered father and usurping uncle, appears to have been lifted from *Hamlet*) and incurring the wrath of the prince's mummified slave, Prem. The film's main variation on the formula is in making one of the archaeologists a scoundrel willing to leave his comrades to their fates; beyond this, it relies on repackaging elements from earlier films. The magic scroll from the original *Mummy* becomes a funeral shroud embroidered with magic spells, while Ardath Bey's all-seeing pool is now a crystal ball used by an evil fortune-teller. If nothing else, *The Mummy's Shroud* manages some inventive death scenes – again indicating the debt that slashers owe to the mummy cycle – and an unusual mummy design. Prem is based directly upon 'EA6704', a Roman-era mummy housed in the British Museum, who has individually-wrapped limbs (common in films but rare in real life) and stylised facial features painted onto his wrappings.[113]

Hammer's fourth and final mummy film, *Blood from the Mummy's Tomb* (1971), adapted Bram Stoker's *The Jewel of Seven Stars*. While it has certain elements that show the influence of previous mummy movies, *Blood from the Mummy's Tomb* stands out as a film drawing on material that is older than the Universal mummy cycle and yet somehow seems comparatively fresh. *The Jewel of Seven Stars* was subsequently adapted by studios other than Hammer as *The Awakening* (1980) and *Bram Stoker's Legend of the Mummy* (1998), the latter film itself begetting *Bram Stoker's Legend of the Mummy 2* (2000). While *The Mummy* and *The Mummy's Hand* established the subgenre, the cycle of *Jewel of Seven Stars* adaptations form a substantial alternative.

OTHER MUMMY FILMS

Beyond these Stoker adaptations, mummy films made outside Universal and Hammer have by and large taken the exploits of Imhotep and Kharis as starting points. A typical example is the 1957 Mexican film *The Aztec Mummy* (*La Momia Azteca*) which moves from Egypt to Mesoamerica but nonetheless borrows much of *The Mummy*'s plot: an Aztec warrior tries to elope with a sacrificial virgin, gets buried alive as punishment, and comes back as a mummy in the twentieth century to hassle his lost love's reincarnation. To be fair, the film does include a somewhat unusual element by pitting the mummy against a band of treasure-seeking gangsters, led by a comic-style villain called the Bat. The film begat a whole cycle of Mexican mummy films, including such genre-crossing entries as *The Robot vs. the Aztec Mummy* (*La Momia Azteca Contra el Robot Humano*, 1957) and *The Wrestling Woman vs. the Aztec Mummy* (*La Lunchadoras Contra la Momia*, 1964).

A case could be made that the living mummy never really formed its own set of rules and conventions comparable to those of the vampire, werewolf or zombie, and that mummy films generally apply Egyptian (or sometimes Mesoamerican) trappings to existing monsters. Ardath Bey recalls prior cinematic magicians. Kharis started his series as a golem, although his later, tantrum-prone incarnation is perhaps closer to Frankenstein's Monster. The Aztec Mummy likewise shows a definite *Frankenstein* influence, grunting and snarling in the manner of Karloff's signature role.

Exploring the further corners of the subgenre we find other monsters that have undergone this mummification process. *Dawn of the Mummy* (1981) applies bandages to the zombies popularised by *Dawn of the Dead* (1978) as a horde of mummies rise from the ground to eat the flesh of grave-robbers and fashion models alike. *Face of the Screaming Werewolf* (1965) involves the resurrection of two Aztec mummies – one of which happens to be the mummy of a werewolf.[114]

Perhaps unsurprisingly, given *The Mummy*'s relation to *Dracula*, a number of its imitators have conflated mummies with vampires. *Love Brides of the Blood Mummy* (*El secreto de la momia Egipcia*, 1973) features a mummy who has women brought to his castle so that he can drink their blood. *The Tomb* (1986) introduces us to Nefratis, illegitimate daughter of Ptolemy, who was buried alive for her blood-drinking habits and resurrected in the present day as a fanged temptress. 'Nefratis was a lot more terrifying than a fellow in a black coat and dinner suit' says *House of Dracula* (1945) star John Carradine in one of the film's genre-referential gags. *Pharaoh's Curse* (1957) uses both the ghost and vampire motifs as the disinterment of Pharaoh Ra-Ha-Teb leads to a round of spiritual possession and blood-drinking. The interplay between vampires and mummies works both ways: *Bram Stoker's Dracula* (1992) interpolates a major plot thread from *The Mummy*, with heroine Mina Murray turning out to be the reincarnation of Dracula's sometime bride, while novelist Anne Rice gave her vampires an Egyptian origin – something reflected in the 2002 film adaptation of her work, *Queen of the Damned*.

Even the monsters of science fiction have been mummified. Television's *Doctor Who* (1963-1989, 2005-) has run a number of episodes involving mummy-like aliens, an early example being the 1967 storyline 'The Tomb of the Cybermen'. Here, a futuristic archaeological expedition opens an extraterrestrial tomb and finds it filled with cyborgs, who break out of a weird structure part sarcophagus, part refrigerator and part honeycomb. Despite its sci-fi trappings the story does not stray far from mummy movie conventions, and even inherits the racial stereotyping of the 1932 film: one of the archaeologists brings a mostly-silent black servant who ends up falling under the sway of the Cybermen.

When mummies are not being conflated with other varieties of monster, they are often playing second fiddle. *Assignment Terror* (*Los Monstros del Terror*, 1969) has alien invaders enlist the help of Earth's indigenous monsters: a vampire, a werewolf, a *Frankenstein*-like monster and a mummy named Pha-Ho-Tep, the last of whom gets almost nothing to do in the film. *The Monster Squad* (1987) sees Dracula attack suburban America with a similar band of Universal-derived monsters in tow, a mummy amongst them. In *The Creeps* (1997) a mad scientist invents a machine that brings literary monsters into the real world, the twist being that each one comes out three feet tall; once again the group includes a mummy, and once again he is cast as a stooge to Dracula.

Crossover films of this sort tend to be comedies, and comedy is another area in which movie mummies have flourished. Some of the earliest films in the subgenre are send-ups, such as *Mummy's Boys* (1936) starring comedians Wheeler and Woolsey and *We Want Our Mummy* (1938) with the Three Stooges; in both of these films the walking mummy turns out to be a disguised crook. Laurel and Hardy also had mummy troubles – although, atypically, not until these comedy legends were dead, and replaced with stand-ins for the cumbersomely-titled *The All New Adventures of Laurel & Hardy in For Love or Mummy* (1999).

Mummy comedies are generally content to simply repeat stereotyped impressions of the Universal series, but one shining exception is *Bubba Ho-Tep* (2002), an offbeat film based on a story by Joe R. Lansdale. The title character is a mummy who dresses like a cowboy and acts like a vampire, draining the souls from his victims; standing against him are a pair of nursing home residents who purport to be Elvis Presley and John F. Kennedy. In its own oddball way, *Bubba Ho-Tep* stays true to *The Mummy*'s themes of death, reincarnation and reminiscence; indeed, it puts them to better use then most of the straight-faced entries in the subgenre.

THE MUMMY AS FRANCHISE

Any studio with sufficient bandages can make a mummy movie, but it is Universal that owns the rights to make a *Mummy* movie. In this era of franchise blockbusters, *The Mummy* remains a viable cinematic brand. While the original Universal *Mummy* series ended in 1955 and the Hammer revival in 1971, the 1990s saw Universal attempt to recreate *The Mummy* for a new generation – although, as it happened, the project took some time before coming to fruition.

At the start of the decade respected author and filmmaker Clive Barker was assigned the job of reimagining *The Mummy*. Barker collaborated with screenwriter Mick Garris and came up with a script involving the birth of a supernatural baby boy, Egyptian gods who turn out to be aliens, and the exploits of a mysterious temptress – who is in fact the same character as the supernatural baby boy, having since grown up and undergone gender reassignment. The script was dismissed as 'perverted' by studio higher-ups.[115]

Joe Dante also attempted to get a version of *The Mummy* off the ground, with a script by John Sayles and the enthusiastic support of Steven Spielberg. This interpretation, later described by Dante as 'satirical' and 'hip', was to have featured a very handsome mummy; again, it was ultimately rejected.[116] George A. Romero was yet another horror auteur

Fig 13: Still from the 2017 Mummy film

who dabbled on the project; he described his vision for The Mummy as being respectful to the 1932 original while adding more action.[117]

The remake of The Mummy was finally released in 1999, directed by Stephen Sommers and starring Brendan Fraser as a roguish hero far brasher than Frank Whemple. Although it revives the characters of Imhotep and Anck-es-en-Amon (or Anck-Su-Namun, as the subtitles render her name) and paraphrases a few snatches from John L. Balderston's script, the film bears little resemblance to its ostensible source. It is somewhat closer in spirit to the comedy-action-spookshow combination of The Mummy's Hand; but at the end of the day, its most obvious inspiration lies with the broad humour, period backdrop and non-stop action of Steven Spielberg's Indiana Jones series.

Gone is Karl Freund's famously restrained resurrection sequence; in its place is a shot of a CGI mummy roaring at the audience. This sums up the general approach of the film, as one of the most subtle works of 1930s horror cinema becomes one of the most gleefully over-the-top 1990s blockbusters.

The film gives Imhotep a raft of superpowers: he regenerates himself through the vampiric process of stealing organs and life-force from archaeologists, turning them into mummified corpses; he has an elemental power over Egypt's sands, conjuring deadly sandstorms and even turning himself into a cloud of dust when he needs to beat a retreat; and his resurrection is marked by five of the ten plagues of Exodus returning to Egypt. The Imhotep of 1932 placed a single Nubian manservant under his control; the Imhotep of 1999 manages to turn a significant chunk of Cairo into chanting somnambulists. The Kharis films contented themselves with just the one mummified henchman; Sommers' climax gives Imhotep a small army of mummies. Instead of a statue raising its arm and a mummy crumbling through dissolving shots, Imhotep's death scene has a ghostly CGI chariot ride away with his immortal spirit. Added to the mix are gunfights, a plane crash, flesh-eating scarabs, elaborate slapstick sequences, trap-filled tombs and an ancient brotherhood of grave-watchers who owe something to the grail guardians from *Indiana Jones and the Last Crusade* (1989). The plot of the original film can just about be glimpsed amongst the additions and reworkings, with Imhotep still striving for reunion with his lost love.

Next came *The Mummy Returns* in 2001, with Sommers, Fraser and company offering more cartoonish japes. The 1932 film's reincarnation subplot – oddly missing from the 1999 remake – returns here, albeit in revised form. The reincarnation of Anck-Su-Namun is cast as a villain, while the series' heroine turns out to have spent a past life as Anck-Su-Namun's rival Nefertiti (in another carefree jumble of famous Egyptian names, Nefertiti is depicted as the daughter of Seti I). The reincarnated Anck-Su-Namun assists in the resurrection of Imhotep; finally reunited with his beloved after his botched efforts in 1932 and 1999, the mummy upgrades his villainous ambitions to world domination. Filling out the colourful rogues' gallery are an evil museum curator with a side in black magic (recalling George Zucco's character in *The Mummy's Hand*), a tribe of pygmy mummies residing in an oddly Amazonian oasis, an army of jackal-headed zombies, and finally the Scorpion King. This minor historical figure is depicted first as a hunky warrior played by Dwayne Johnson and later as a CGI half-man, half-scorpion monster.

The Mummy Returns was followed by a tie-in cartoon series that ran from 2001 to 2003, while Dwayne Johnson's character was re-used for the campy sword-and-sorcery spin-off *The Scorpion King* (2002) – a film which went on to inspire sequels of its own. Egypt having apparently been plundered dry, the franchise moved to East Asia with *The Mummy: Tomb of the Dragon Emperor* (2008). Here, an undead Chinese despot rampages to Tibet and back before starting a CGI battle between animated terracotta soldiers and an army of skeletons; yetis and a three-headed dragon also turn up for good measure.

As the twenty-first century reached its second decade, Hollywood realised the potential for shared universe blockbusters. Marvel Studios led the way with superhero crossovers such as *The Avengers* (2012) but as Universal had explored similar territory back in the 1940s with the likes of *Frankenstein Meets the Wolf Man* (1943), it was inevitable that the superhero smashes would be followed by monster mashes. And so 2017 saw another remake of *The Mummy*, billed as the first in a proposed line of 'Dark Universe' films that would re-introduce the classic Universal monsters to the screen in new forms, ready to rub shoulders with one another. Directed by veteran blockbuster scribe Alex Kurtzman and starring Tom Cruise, the 2017 *Mummy* turned out to be a box-office disappointment, ending the Dark Universe before it was able to truly get started.[118]

This remake comes across as an awkward hodge-podge unable to develop its own identity. Half the time it is ticking boxes for possible sequels and spin-offs: both hero and villain fall into the hands of a monster-hunting organisation run by Dr. Jekyll, a plot element that was clearly intended to provide a linking device with future Dark Universe films. The other half of the time it is cribbing from earlier films, as when Tom Cruise's dead friend is resurrected as gross-out comic relief in a direct lift from *An American Werewolf in London* (1981). Eschewing the period settings of the Sommers versions, the film takes place in the present day and manages to work the destruction of antiquities by ISIS into its storyline – although this necessitates a plot contrivance to explain how an Egyptian tomb ended up in Iraq. The mummy this time is that of Ahmanet, an ancient sorceress buried alive for killing her family and summoning Set (dubiously identified as the Egyptian god of death).

Despite the film's flaws, Sofia Boutella leaves an impression as the revived Ahmanet. Her striking appearance – lank hair, tattered wrappings and skin inscribed with lettering – shows the influence of Japanese horror films and marks a worthy addition to mummy-movie iconography. In a possible attempt to avoid charges of cultural prejudice, the film gives Ahmanet an army of European mummies – namely, undead Knights Templar – who provide a number of fetchingly Gothic scenes. None of this is enough to salvage the 2017 *Mummy*, however.

Not all of The *Mummy*'s retellings occurred onscreen: its story has also been reworked multiple times in print. The film's first prose adaptation was a short story by James Whitlatch, published in the January 1933 edition of *Mystery Magazine*.[119] Narrated by the character of Muller, this version of the story begins after Anck-es-en-Amon's tomb has been excavated, with Muller briefly describing Imhotep's disinterment in past tense towards the end. As well as compressing the narrative, Whitlatch's story prefigures the 1999 remake by giving Imhotep the ability to turn his victims into lifeless mummies with a touch: Joseph Whemple, the museum guard and the archaeologist Pearson all suffer this fate, while Helen only narrowly avoids receiving a kiss of death.

The film did not receive a full-length novelisation until 1977, when Berkley Medallion put out a series of books retelling Universal classics, all written under the house name of Carl Dreadstone.[120] The adaptation of *The Mummy* shifts the supernatural focus away from Ardath Bey (who barely registers as anything more than a shadowy background presence) and towards Helen. The reincarnated heroine is inserted into the prologue, where she tosses and turns in her bed at the precise moment that Imhotep is revived over in Egypt; later scenes have her talking about past lives in her sleep and visiting ancient Egypt in an out-of-body experience. Also notable is the author's attempt to incorporate actual Egyptian history by conflating the film's Anck-es-en-Amon (here spelled Ankhesenamen) with her historical namesake. The novel confirms that Helen's past self is indeed *the* Ankhesenamen, daughter of Akhenaten and Nefertiti, bride of Tutankhamun; her tragic affair with Imhotep now takes place against a backdrop of Egyptian power politics, with the succession of Pharaoh Ay and strained relations with the Hittites.

The twenty-first century has seen further novels tying in with *The Mummy*, this time offering high-concept twists on the film's story. Between 2001 and 2002 Scholastic published a series of six children's books by Larry Mike Garmon in which modern-day teenagers Joe, Bob and Nina accidentally transport various Universal monsters into the real world using an experimental 3D movie projector. The youngsters then have to figure out which members of their local community are monsters in disguise, all the while indulging in the sort of intertextual japery popularised by *Scream* (1996) and *Buffy the Vampire Slayer* (1997-2003). The fourth volume in Garmon's series, *Book of the Dead*, sees Ardath Bey infiltrate the high school and try to raise Anck-es-en-Amon (here spelled Anck-Su-Namun) by sacrificing Nina in a climax that owes more to the 1999 film than the 1932 original. The mummy gets another new superpower in this novel, being able to bring Egyptian statuary to life.

A few years later Dark Horse Books published six further novels tying in with the Universal classics, this time aimed at adult horror fans and with a different author writing each volume. Amongst these was *The Mummy: Dark Resurrection* (2007), penned by John Michael Curlovich under the pseudonym Michael Paine. While most of the books in the series are sequels to their respective films, Curlovich instead retells the basic narrative of *The Mummy* with a number of new twists. Set in the twenty-first century, the novel replaces the English Whemple family of the film with the Brandts, a wealthy Pittsburgh dynasty, and establishes a contrast between crass modern materialism and ancient Egyptian mysticism. The main character is Joshua Brandt, one of the few decent members of the family, whose father went missing after violating the tomb of Imhotep; meanwhile, the spirit of Anck-es-en-Amon (here spelled Ankh-es-en-Amun) now lives inside Joshua's sister Stephanie, a mental patient with multiple personality disorder.

Echoing the 1977 novelisation, Curlovich ties the character of Imhotep to the historical personage of the same name. The novel establishes that Imhotep's deification led to him being periodically resurrected throughout history – thereby allowing his anachronistic dalliance with Ankh-es-en-Amun. In this version of the story Imhotep/Ardath Bey has the ability to raise the recently-dead as zombies, which he uses to pick off the Brandt family through a macabre domino effect as each new victim rises to slay the next. *Dark Resurrection* ultimately places the plot of *The Mummy* between old and modern varieties of horror story: the former is represented by the classic Gothic motif of the cursed family, the latter by the no-holds-barred violence, zombie imagery and bleak ending (Josh loses his mind after Imhotep forces Stephanie to birth an inhuman child) that recall 'splatter' fiction of the 1980s and after.[121]

THE BROADER PICTURE

All of the above is merely the tip of the pyramid. The central motifs of *The Mummy* have spread far outside of cinema and come to permeate popular media in general.

The horror comics that sparked moral panic in the 1950s used mummies as stock characters, some of the many examples being *Beware*'s Ak-Ahmen, *Spook*'s Ramzu XI, *The Beyond*'s Uer-Moa, *Forbidden Worlds*' Rhames-Tut-Arkham, *The Thing*'s Rah Kamsis and *Web of Mystery*'s Kali-Dahn; particularly unscrupulous titles passed off their Universal-inspired strips as 'true tales' of the supernatural.[122] In the world of animation, mummies have been depicted variously as villainous henchmen (*Drak Pack*, 1980), big lugs (*Hotel Transylvania*, 2012), dumpy high school nerds (*Gravedale High*, 1990) and even superheroes (*Mummies Alive!*, 1997). The opening sequence to *Scooby-Doo and Scrappy-Doo* (1979-80) has Scrappy unravelling a mummy to nothingness by tugging on a loose bandage, an image that now rivals Imhotep's resurrection in terms of iconic status.

Pan's People, Daft Punk, the Backstreet Boys, Howard Jones and Katy Perry have all used dancing mummies in music videos or live performances, while a garage punk band called the Mummies swathed themselves in bandages as a group motif. Innumerable video games feature mummy characters, up to and including a mummy-themed Pokémon named Cofagrigus. *Dungeons & Dragons*, the role-playing game more generally associated with elves, dwarfs and orcs, has included mummies as part of its bestiary since its debut in 1974. In the late 1980s and early 1990s General Mills manufactured a breakfast cereal called Fruity Yummy Mummy – which, as a cartoon mummy in the accompanying advert assured children, 'makes your tummy go yummy'. At around the same time kids in Britain were eating yogurt from mummy-themed pots, courtesy of St Ivel's 'Fiendish Feet' brand. Mattel produces a mummy fashion doll named Cleo de Nile, part of the successful Monster High line. And so on.

It is possible that some of these may have existed even had *The Mummy* never been made. After all, as noted near the start of this book, Walt Disney had put funny cartoon mummies onscreen a year before Boris Karloff was wrapped up to play Imhotep. Nonetheless, it seems safe to say that the bulk of pop culture's living mummy imagery was inspired either directly or indirectly by *The Mummy*.

On the most basic level, Universal's film cemented the concept of the mummy not as a human corpse, not even as a historical artefact, but as a monster – a class of supernatural entity comparable to the vampire or werewolf. On a broader level it helped to establish an imaginary vision of ancient Egypt: Imhotep and Anck-es-en-Amon were followed onto the screens by the likes of Kharis, Klaris, Ananka, Prem, Ra-Ha-

Teb, Pha-Ho-Tep, Nefratis and Ahmanet, to name but a few; enough phony pharaohs, priests and princesses to fill an entire dynasty. This fantasy Egypt provides a number of accessories for the movie mummy – and mummies require such accessories if they are to prosper.

Some monsters can benefit from multiplication; this is why films have created underground communities of vampires, and zombie hordes big enough to bring about the apocalypse. Mummies, however, have shown that they benefit from addition: the living mummy is ultimately an ingredient, one that needs other, similarly strong ingredients to survive. Some of the more obvious ingredients are curses, mythology, archaeological discoveries and ancient courtly intrigue; other, less obvious ingredients include robots, Mexican wrestlers, the Three Stooges, Count Dracula, Doctor Who and Elvis Presley, all of whom have tangled with mummies at one point or another.

This reliance on additional ingredients explains why the various remakes and retellings of *The Mummy* – such as Clive Barker's gender-bending science fiction, Stephen Sommers' cartoonish romp and John Michael Curlovich's splatter novelisation – depart so drastically from the original film. Yet even so, much of the 1932 film's central iconography remains visible across these later incarnations.

The creative talent behind *The Mummy* borrowed liberally from a strain of nineteenth- and early twentieth-century supernatural fiction dealing with mummies, reincarnation and Egyptian mysticism. At the same time, they distilled this influence into a potent concoction of iconography, the essential spirit of which has survived through generations' worth of re-interpretations.

FOOTNOTES

111. While not particularly logical, the idea of a superhumanly strong mummy does have precedent in weird fiction, as one of the mummies in Théophile Gautier's 'The Mummy's Foot' proclaims that 'my flesh is solid as basalt, my bones are bars of steel'.
112. Kinsey, W., *Hammer Films: The Bray Studios Years* (Reynolds & Hearn, London, 2002) p144
113. Kinsey, W., *Hammer Films: The Bray Studios Years* (Reynolds & Hearn, London, 2002) p348; Coniam, M., *Egyptomania Goes to the Movies: From Archaeology to Popular Craze to Hollywood Fantasy* (McFarland & Company, Jefferson, 2017) p64

114. *Face of the Screaming Werewolf* was the result of US filmmaker Jerry Warren editing together two unrelated films from Mexico: one was *The Aztec Mummy*, the other a Lon Chaney Jr. werewolf comedy called *La Casa del Terror* (1959). See Senn, B., *The Werewolf Filmography: 300+ Movies* (McFarland, Jefferson, 2017) p86.
115. Stokes, P and Stokes, S., 'Film Projects - Cooler', CliveBarker.info, https://www.clivebarker.info/filmsold.html
116. Klen., J., 'Interview: Joe Dante', AVClub.com, https://www.avclub.com/joe-dante-1798208125
117. Romero, G. A., *George A. Romero: Interviews* (University Press of Mississippi, Jackson, 2011) p127
118. Donaldson, K., 'Where Universal went wrong with their Dark Universe and how they can fix it'. *Syfy.com*. https://www.syfy.com/syfywire/where-universal-went-wrong-with-their-dark-universe-and-how-they-can-fix-it
119. The story is reprinted in Riley, P. J. (ed.) *The Mummy* (MagicImage Filmbooks, Absecon, 1989).
120. In most cases 'Carl Dreadstone' was either Ramsey Campbell or Walter Harris. However, *The Mummy*'s novelisation is an exception, and the author behind the pseudonym is unknown. See Langford, D., 'Carl Dreadstone', *SF-Encyclopedia.com*, http://www.sf-encyclopedia.com/entry/dreadstone_carl.
121. The splatter novels of the 1980s had their roots in a wider paperback horror boom that can be traced back to Ira Levin's *Rosemary's Baby* (1967), a story of supernatural pregnancy that is echoed by the climax to *The Mummy: Dark Resurrection*. See Hendrix, G., *Paperbacks from Hell: The Twisted History of '70s and '80s Horror Fiction* (Quirk Books, Philadelphia, 2017).
122. See Banes, S. (ed.), *Classic Monsters of Pre-Code Horror Comics: Mummies* (Yoe Books, San Diego, 2017).

Conclusion

In Théophile Gautier's story the modern man who bought the mummy's foot fell asleep and dreamed. He dreamed of being visited by an ancient Egyptian princess named Hermonthis before journeying to the world of immortal pharaohs.

Over December 1932 and January 1933, something similar played out on a larger scale. The treasures of Tutankhamun had been unpacked and examined by the public, directly or through reproduced images. Now it was time to dream. Dark rooms filled with flickering images of age-old artefacts, and a pharaoh, and a princess, and a mummy.

Sometimes the dream was a nightmare. A man buried alive, dug up as a desiccated corpse, and allowed to walk again; a young man falling into insane laughter; an older man perishing from black magic, a woman about to be slain and turned into a mummy. Other times it was a sad dream, full of loss and longing.

Dreams are often formed of dredged-up memories. This dream contained memories of old stories: stories of immortal Ayesha courting her groom-to-be, of lot no. 249 sliding through the shadows of Oxford, of Tera regaining her old body at the Great Experiment's close, of Tuthmosis pining for his lost love Atma. The memories blurred in and out of one another: the mummy looked like Frankenstein's Monster, but he acted like Dracula. Or was he the man of clay, the golem?

Above all, it is a recurring dream. Its principal characters come back to us time and again. The names change: sometimes they are Imhotep and Anck-es-en-Amon, other times Kharis and Ananka, but they are always recognisable. David Manners is sometimes Brendan Fraser; Edward Van Sloan is sometimes Peter Cushing – and both of them are Van Helsing. Helen Grosvenor was not the only person to be reincarnated.

Dream-Egypt is a strange place, different from real Egypt. The Valley of the Kings looks like Red Rock Canyon; perhaps Tom Tyler is having a gunfight with outlaws around the corner. The pharaoh buries his daughter in Weimar Germany. Scooby-Doo is chased down an eternal corridor. If the dream captivates us, we will not object.

Children do not object as they play with their mummy toys and watch their mummy cartoons and eat their mummy confections. When Halloween arrives they may even become mummies themselves, through a process less harrowing than the one undertaken by Imhotep. Kharis sought tana leaves; his little descendants prefer candy corn.

We wake up from the dream and leave the darkened room, but the memories remain. The mummy who walked from his sarcophagus is still out there somewhere. He has joined the vampires, the zombies, the knife-gloved killers, the ghost girls in TV sets and all those other monsters we made so that we could find comfort in our own fears.

Before long it will be time for us to head back to that darkened room. We shall once again visit the dream-Egypt where mummies walk and princesses are reborn. Some old acquaintances will be there: Imhotep, who had been Kallikrates, Cagliostro and Tuthmosis; Anck-es-en-Amon, who had been Atma, Tera and Hermonthis.

We will recognise them, of course.

'In many forms shall we return…'

Bibliography

Adair, G., *Alfred Hitchcock: Filming Our Fears* (Oxford University Press, Oxford, 2002)

Allen, S. J., *Tutankhamun's Tomb: The Thrill of Discovery* (Metropolitan Museum of Art, New York, 2006)

Ashley, M., *The History of the Science Fiction Magazine, Part One: 1926-1935* (New English Library, London, 1974)

Assmann, J., *Death and Salvation in Ancient Egypt* (Cornell University Press, Ithaca, 2005)

Atkins, R., *Guest Parking: Zita Johann* (BearManor Media, Albany, 2015)

Baigent, M. and Leigh, R., *The Elixir and the Stone: A History of Magic and Alchemy* (Viking, London, 1997)

Banes, S. (ed.), *Classic Monsters of Pre-Code Horror Comics: Mummies* (Yoe Books, San Diego, 2017)

Bard, K. A., *Encyclopedia of the Archaeology of Ancient Egypt* (Routledge, London, 1999)

Berenstein, R. J., *Attack of the Leading Ladies: Gender, Sexuality, and Spectatorship in Classic Horror Cinema* (Columbia University Press, New York, 1996)

Blanco, J. (ed.) *Clothing and Fashion: American Fashion from Head to Toe* (ABC-CLIO, Santa Barbara, 2016)

Bogdan, H. and Starr, M. P. in *Aleister Crowley and Western Esotericism* (Oxford University Press, Oxford, 2012)

Budge, E. A. W., *The Egyptian Book of the Dead* (Penguin, London, 2008)

Budge, E. A. W., *Egyptian Tales & Romances* (Thornton Butterworth, London, 1935)

Bunson, M., *Encyclopedia of Ancient Egypt* (Facts On File, Inc, New York, 2002)

Clarens, C., *An Illustrated History of the Horror Film* (G. P. Putnam's Sons, New York, 1967)

Coniam, M., *Egyptomania Goes to the Movies: From Archaeology to Popular Craze to Hollywood Fantasy* (McFarland & Company, Jefferson, 2017)

Cumming, M., *The Carlyle Encyclopedia* (Fairleigh Dickinson University Press, Madison, 2004)

Daniels, L., *Fear: A History of Horror in the Mass Media* (Granada Publishing, St Albans, 1975)

Day, J., *The Mummy's Curse: Mummymania in the English-Speaking World* (Routledge, Abingdon, Oxon, 2006)

Dodson, A. and Hilton, D., *The Complete Royal Families of Ancient Egypt* (Thames & Hudson, London, 2004)

Dreadstone, C., *The Mummy* (Berkley Publishing Corporation, New York, 1977)

Essman, S., *Jack Pierce: The Man Behind the Monsters* (Visionary Media, Glendora, 2000)

Everson, W. K., *Classics of the Horror Film: From the Days of the Silent Film to The Exorcist* (The Citadel Press, Secaucus, 1974)

Frank, A., *Monsters & Vampires* (Octopus Books, London, 1976)

Garmon, L. M., *Universal Monsters #4: The Mummy: Book of the Dead* (Scholastic, New York, 2002)

Genini, R., *Theda Bara: A Biography of the Silent Screen Vamp, with a Filmography* (McFarland & Company, Jefferson, 1996)

Gervaso, R., *Cagliostro: A Biography* (Victor Gollancz Limited, London, 1974)

Grant, B. K., *Planks of Reason: Essays on the Horror Film* (Scarecrow Press, Metuchen, 1984)

Haining, P., (ed.), *The Mummy: Stories of the Living Corpse* (Severn House, New York, 1989)

Hankey, J., *A Passion for Egypt: Arthur Welgall, Tutankhamun and the Curse of the Pharaohs* (Tauris Parke Paperbacks, London, 2007)

Hartley, C., *A Case for Reincarnation* (St Edmundsbury Press, Bury St Edmunds, 1985)

Hendrix, G., *Paperbacks from Hell: The Twisted History of '70s and '80s Horror Fiction* (Quirk Books, Philadelphia, 2017)

Johnson, T., *Censored Screams: The British Ban on Hollywood Horror in the Thirties* (McFarland & Company, Jefferson, 1997)

Kinsey, W., *Fantastic Films of the Decades, Volume 1: The Silent Era* (Peveril Publishing, Barnby, 2015)

Kinsey, W., *Fantastic Films of the Decades, Volume 2: The 30s* (Peveril Publishing, Barnby, 2015) pp29, 33

Kinsey, W., *Hammer Films: The Bray Studios Years* (Reynolds & Hearn, London, 2002)

Kuhn, A., *An Everyday Magic: Cinema and Cultural Memory* (I. B. Tauris, London, 2002)

Leca, A-P., *The Cult of the Immortal: Mummies and the Ancient Way of Death* (Granada, St Albans, 1983)

Mank, G. W., *Women in Horror Films, 1930s* (McFarland & Company, Jefferson, 1999)

Marriott, J. and Newman, K. (eds), *Horror: The Definitive Guide to the Cinema of Fear* (Andre Deutch, London, 2006)

Matthews, M. E., *Fear Itself: Horror on Screen and in Reality During the Depression and World War II* (McFarland & Company, Jefferson, 2009)

Osborne, C., *The Opera Lover's Companion* (Yale University Press, New Hale, 2004)

Paine, M., *The Mummy: Dark Resurrection* (Dark Horse Books, Milwaukie, 2007)

Peirse, A., *After Dracula: The 1930s Horror Film* (I. B. Tauris, London, 2013)

Pringle, H., *The Mummy Congress: Science, Obsession, and the Everlasting Dead* (Hyperion Books, New York, 2001)

Rigby, J., *American Gothic: Six Decades of Classic American Horror Cinema* (Signum Books, Cambridge, 2017)

Riley, P. J., *Cagliostro, The King of the Dead: An Alternate History for Classic Film Monsters* (BearManor Media, Albany, 2010)

Riley, P. J., *Dracula Starring Lon Chaney: An Alternate History for Classic Film Monsters* (BearManor Media, Albany, 2010)

Riley, P. J., *The Mummy* (MagicImage Filmbooks, Absecon, 1989)

Robins, G., *Women in Ancient Egypt* (The British Museum Press, London, 1993)

Romero, G. A., *George A. Romero: Interviews* (University Press of Mississippi, Jackson, 2011)

Senn, B., *The Werewolf Filmography: 300+ Movies* (McFarland & Company, Jefferson, 2017)

Shaheen, J. G., *Reel Bad Arabs: How Hollywood Vilifies a People* (Arris Books, Moreton-in-Marsh, 2003)

Shaw, I. and Nicholson, P., *British Museum Dictionary of Ancient Egypt* (BCA, London, 1995)

Skal, D. J., *Hollywood Gothic: The Tangled Web of Dracula from Novel to Stage to Screen* (W. W. Norton, New York, 2004)

Skal, D. J., *The Monster Show: A Cultural History of Horror* (Penguin Books, London, 1994)

Smith, S. T., *Box Office Archaeology: Refining Hollywood's Portrayals of the Past* (Routledge, Abingdon, 2016)

Solomon, J., *The Ancient World in the Cinema* (Yale University Press, New Haven, 2001)

Spadoni, R., *Uncanny Bodies: The Coming of Sound Film and the Origins of the Horror Genre* (University of California Press, Berkeley, 2007)

Spencer, A. J., *Death in Ancient Egypt* (Penguin Books, London, 1982)

Stoker, B., *The Jewel of Seven Stars* (Oxford University Press, Oxford, 1996)

Takács, S. A., *Vestal Virgins, Sibyls, and Matrons: Women in Roman Religion* (University of Texas Press, Austin, 2008)

Tyson, D., *The Dream World of H. P. Lovecraft: His Life, His Demons, His Universe* (Llewellyn Publications, Woodbury, 2010)

Weaver, T. Brunas, M., and Brunas, J., *Universal Horrors: The Studio's Classic Films, 1931–1946* (McFarland & Company, Jefferson, 2007)

www.ingramcontent.com/pod-product-compliance
Ingram Content Group UK Ltd.
Pitfield, Milton Keynes, MK11 3LW, UK
UKHW021557230326
469232UK00007B/212